T0155052

Naked Angels
The Issues Projects

Naked Angels
THE ISSUES PROJECTS
Collected Plays

Edited by
Mark Armstrong and
Geoffrey Nauffts

Playscripts, Inc.

New York, NY

Published by Playscripts, Inc.
450 Seventh Avenue, Suite 809
New York, New York, 10123
www.playscripts.com

Cover design by Tom Slaughter and Noah Press
Text design and layout by Jason Pizzarello

First Edition: September 2009
10 9 8 7 6 5 4 3 2 1

ISBN-13: 978-0-9819099-1-2

Library of Congress Cataloging-in-Publication Data

Naked angels issues projects : collected plays / edited by Mark Armstrong and Geoffrey Nauffts. -- 1st ed.
    p. cm.
  ISBN 978-0-9819099-1-2 (pbk.)
  1. American drama--21st century. I. Armstrong, Mark, 1972- II. Nauffts, Geoffrey.
  PS634.2.N35 2009
  812'.608--dc22

                    2009013185

In loving memory of Jenifer Estess.

contents

foreword

Naked Angels is a theater company made up of a ragtag collective of writers, actors, directors and designers. For many of the artists represented here, the company was a beginning. To careers, to relationships, friendships and loyalties all born out of a shared place and time. The Issues Projects were arguably Naked Angels' most successful and identifiable programming. For many years our home was a warehouse on West 17th street in Manhattan. The rent was minimal, as the uncle of one of our founders owned the building. Now it is expensive residential lofts, with a giant camera emporium where most of the plays in this book were first mounted. We may well have been influenced by our members' knowledge of companies like Joint Stock, in England, where David Hare, Caryl Churchill, Howard Brenton and others created a kind of theater that insisted on being part of the national dialogue. (Harder to do here, where theater is more marginalized.) To reach further back, but closer to home, Harold Clurman's Group Theatre, mounting, say, Clifford Odets' *Waiting for Lefty* also figured into the model of a useful living theater, as did the Federal Theatre Project.

The company would gather to decide on an issue of sufficient weight as to merit an entire evening of plays devoted to the subject. It was dangerous territory, simply because so much of what passes for political theater ends up merely being an attenuated form of earnest preaching to a well-intentioned choir. 'Perhaps that's enough?' I used to think. 'Is it enough to merely remind ourselves that our comfortable lives here in Manhattan are marred by the travesties of the larger world outside?' Now, an older playwright, I am at peace with that particular capitulation to the verities, and also with the value of comedy as weapon, much more so, in fact, than tragedy, at least, say, in short ten-minute theatrical bursts.

Context and chronology are everything: When The Issues Projects first began, the elder George Bush was in office and we had seamlessly moved from the febrile inequities and outrages of the Reagan era, into a stultifying patrician torpor under George Bush Senior, a torpor that only further emboldened the far-right evangelical movement to interfere in bedrooms, courtrooms, and classrooms across the land. Capitalism continued, and thanks to Reagan, now virtually unfettered by regulation, coupled with a drive to break organized labor were also notable pinpricks to a national complacency. Yet those pinpricks mostly went unheard and unfelt. Unexamined. The 'business-first, business is the business of America' sensibility gave rise to energy policies we are paying for today, as did a disastrous inattention to the environment. Wall Street forgot 1987 and our need to buy silenced our qualms. So, the world being what it is, we had plenty of issues to choose from, and we raised money for the issue at hand; Amnesty International, for instance. There: Something practical, a practical good as well as a theatrical one: Benefits for causes, attached to an evening of plays to heighten awareness. Not a bad legacy for a theater company. I think, more than anything, this volume is a useful record of a time and its issues, from the right to privacy, to torture, to the environment, to homelessness. Of course nothing was solved on that stage; but is anything ever solved on any stage? We now live with another two new wars, rising homelessness, and a shattered economy; the endgame of corporate greed. There is no room to be apolitical anymore; America has at last woken from a decades old slumber.

Short plays are, I think, acts of compression, and as such have a different music to them: staccato and vivid. They require a frisson. Personally, I honed some skills in writing brief pieces. On how to focus a pin-light for a very brief time at high focus, and find a combination of uncomfortable, recognizable behavioral truth, and still make something lecture-free. No time for leisurely Chekhovian dying falls. At their most powerful, say, Harold Pinter's two succinct masterpieces, *One for the Road*, and *Mountain Language*, or Beckett's *Catastrophe* the plays are not constricted by their brevity; rather, they are made more powerful because of it.

I'm proud of the work we did, the ambition of it, the goodness at hand, in mostly young playwrights, actors, and directors not turning away from the world we lived in then, and still live in now. Most of life is compromise, coarsening, and the banking of fires. These plays burn very bright for a very little while. If nothing else, they remind one of how much is still to be done, and how the theater can help do it, at least, incrementally. In short, short increments. This is not nothing.

—**Jon Robin Baitz**

editors' notes

Over two decades ago, I stumbled upon a disparate group of actors, writers, directors and designers. They welcomed me in, we built a theater on West 17th Street, and my life as an artist began. In assembling this collection, paying homage to what is perhaps our signature work, I'm reminded of the incredible impact Naked Angels has had on my artistic development. And I am but one of the many hundreds who have been well-served by their time spent with the company. This book and the body of work it represents would not have been possible without the tireless efforts of former board chair Tessa Blake and former artistic director Tim Ransom who truly got the ball rolling. Thanks also goes out to everyone who ever helped produce or participated in an Issues Project over the years. The following individuals and organizations are but a few of the many who were instrumental in helping to secure Naked Angels' place in theater history: Jace Alexander, Allure Magazine, Amnesty International, Alicia Arinella, Brady Center to Prevent Gun Violence, Christian Dior Perfumes, Covenant House, Liz Diamond, Andy Donald, Paul S. Eckstein, Beth Emelson, Tamlyn Freund, Jill Garland, Marin Gazzaniga, Jenny Gersten, Paul Gruen, Julianne Hoffenberg, Rachael Horovitz, Kathleen A. Houle, Iris House, Kourtney Keaton, Toni Kotite, Charle Landry, Victoria Leacock, Bruce MacVittie, Karl Mann, John M. McCormack, Jack Merrill, Lynn Nottage, Pippin Parker, Mary Elizabeth Peters, Frank Pugliese, The Rosenstiel Foundation, Michael Ryall, and Fisher Stevens.

—**Geoffrey Nauffts**

Eleven years ago, before I moved to New York, I was direct-ing a play in my native Minnesota. While researching the work, I discovered the play had recently been presented at a hip New York theater called Naked Angels and Jacqueline Ken-nedy Onassis had attended a performance. That sounded like everything I imagined living in New York would be like—edgy, important, historical. Years later, I'm surprised and very hon-ored to find myself playing a small role in documenting the great history of Naked Angels and their important work. My thanks to the entire Naked Angels organization, who worked over several years in partnering with Playscripts on this volume. In particular, the passion of Geoffrey Nauffts, Robbie Baitz and Tom Slaughter for Naked Angels has been infectious. For Play-scripts, Jason Pizzarello, Kimberly Lew, Erin Austin, and Les Hunt-er really made this book happen.

—**Mark Armstrong**

homeless

Bruce MacVittie and Willie Garson in *Baby Gators*
Naked Angels at The Coast Theater in Los Angeles City (1993).

BABY GATORS
by Pippin Parker

BIOGRAPHY

Pippin Parker is a founding member and former Artistic Director of Naked Angels and was Co-Artistic Director of the Democracy Issues Project. As a writer, his plays include *Anesthesia, Assisted Living,* and an assortment of one acts, which have been produced in New York and Los Angeles. Television credits include the animated series *The Tick* and *Pocoyo.*

He was director and dramaturg of the original production of George Packer's *Betrayed* at Culture Project in New York (Lortel Award for Outstanding Play 2008), subsequently staged at The Kennedy Center in Washington, DC.

He is currently Chair of the graduate playwriting department at the New School for Drama (New School University) in New York and is a Writers Guild of America, East council member.

ACKNOWLEDGMENTS

Baby Gators was first produced by Naked Angels at The Space in New York City as a part of *Homeless* on February 27, 1989. It was conceived/produced by Charle Landy and Michael Ryall with the following cast:

Paul S. Eckstein
Bruce MacVittie

And the following production staff:

Producer...Julianne Hoffenberg
Scenic Design...Chris Kondek

CAST OF CHARACTERS

CAL
TAFT

BABY GATORS

Black. Silence. Poing. A tear of water landing in a small puddle far below.
Poing. Another.

A slant of light. TAFT *carries* CAL *on. Props him against a wall. Sits*
next to him. After a minute:

CAL. Fuckin' cold.

TAFT. Fuckin' hungry.

CAL. Fuckin' tired.

TAFT. Fuckin' wet down here.

*(*CAL *pulls out a mangled pack of cigarettes. Searches his pockets for a*
match. Can't find one. Desperate. Remembers. Reaches inside his pants.
Pulls out a book of matches. Lights triumphantly.)

TAFT. Gimme one.

*(*CAL *ignores him.)*

TAFT. Lemme have one.

CAL. No.

TAFT. One stoag.

CAL. Nickel.

TAFT. Fuck you, nickel. *(Pause.)* Split it.

CAL. Five cents.

TAFT. A *drag.*

*(*CAL *ignores.* TAFT *grabs it from his mouth.)*

TAFT. *(Inhaling deeply:)* Nickel my ugly jock.

CAL. You know you could use some social skills.

TAFT. Pity.

CAL. Fuckin' animal.

TAFT. Bingo.

CAL. Greedy animal. Thief.

TAFT. Call a cop.

CAL. Getajob.

TAFT. Lick my dick.

CAL. Dream about it.

TAFT. Break my heart.

CAL. *(Sniffing:)* Smells like shit.

TAFT. Change your diaper.

CAL. *(Berating himself:)* Slob!

TAFT. You smell.

CAL. Take a walk.

TAFT. *(Starting to get up:)* Watch me go.

CAL. Hey. Looky what I still got.

> *(*TAFT *swipes for the cigarettes,* CAL *pulls them away in time. He laughs weakly.* TAFT *sits back down. Long pause.)*

TAFT. What time is it?

CAL. Starving…

TAFT. Two o'clock…

CAL. Only nine, maybe ten…

TAFT. Two o'clock, take a walk.

CAL. Freezing…

TAFT. Two o-five, dumpster dive.

CAL. If I'm still alive. Feel like shit.

TAFT. Wait a bit. Two o'clock.

CAL. Cold down here.

TAFT. Raining out there.

CAL. Snowing.

TAFT. Sleeting filthy slush out there.

CAL. Need a bed.

TAFT. Bed and bread.

CAL. Need a home.

TAFT. On your own.

CAL. Fuck that. I'm a family man.

TAFT. Born and bred.

CAL. Come from a long line of families.

TAFT. Who don't?

CAL. Families all the way back to the Garden of Eden.

TAFT. Quit whining. Fuckin' crybaby.

CAL. Adam and Eve.

TAFT. Sodom and Gomorrah. Piece a shit city.

CAL. Family man. Turkey dinners.

TAFT. Animals eating animals.

CAL. Called it home.

TAFT. Call *this* home. This is *it*.

CAL. I'm sick.

TAFT. Baby alligators.

CAL. Wish I had something to throw up.

TAFT. Flushed me down when I got too big.

CAL. You ate too much.

TAFT. Into the sewers.

CAL. Waist deep in waste.

TAFT. Eating garbage. Grew up mean and ugly.

CAL. Ugly reptile. They don't know you now.

TAFT. Used to be cute.

CAL. Coochee-coo little gator. Play nice with mother.

TAFT. Coochee-coo little beast. Don't eat your brother.

CAL. *(Pause.)* ...home...

TAFT. Gimme a break.

CAL. Gimme a mother mother mother *fucking* break.

TAFT. What's your problem?

CAL. I don't feel so good!

TAFT. So shut *up*. You'll eat. Two o'clock.

CAL. Need something now. Doctor.

TAFT. Doctor Jack Daniels Black Label Lynchburg Tennessee.

CAL. Medicine.

TAFT. Nothing a leftover grilled cheese won't cure. Side of slaw...

CAL. I'm sweating.

TAFT. Don't sweat it.

CAL. Fucking eighteen degrees and I'm sweating.

TAFT. Light a smoke.

CAL. Not yet.

TAFT. C'mon. Gimme one.

CAL. Gotta save 'em

TAFT. For what?

CAL. For later. For tonight, tomorrow.

TAFT. For right fucking now.

CAL. And forever.

TAFT. I can't stand it!

CAL. *You* can't stand it?

TAFT. You got it.

CAL. I got *nothing.* I got *shit.* I'm fucking *tired* and *wet* and *cold* and *hungry* and *sick.*

TAFT. I know.

> *(Takes off his coat. Puts it around* CAL.*)*

CAL. You know.

TAFT. I'm sorry.

CAL. You can't help.

TAFT. Get you some food.

> *(He stands. Stomps his feet to warm them up. Starts to go.)*

CAL. *(Scared:)* Where you going?

TAFT. Nowhere.

> *(He sits back down. Pause.)*

CAL. Fucking clammy swamp down here.

TAFT. Good place for alligators.

CAL. Human couldn't survive here a day.

TAFT. Well then, we should do okay.

CAL. Feel like a dying rat.

TAFT. Blinded bat.

CAL. Skinny fuckin' cat.

TAFT. Shit in a hat.

CAL. Think about that. *(He giggles, weak. Long pause.)* Gotta lie down.

TAFT. Stretch out on the ground.

> *(CAL lies down. Closes his eyes. Coughs. Curls.)*

CAL. Get some food later?

TAFT. Go to sleep, baby gator.

> *(CAL coughs again. Wheezes. TAFT looks at him. Takes his coat back. Shoves his hands into his pockets.)*
>
> *(Lights.)*

End of Play

the
naked
truth

FOUR MONOLOGUES
by Jon Robin Baitz

BIOGRAPHY

Jon Robin Baitz is the author of a number of plays including *The Substance of Fire, A Fair Country, Ten Unknowns, Mizlansky/Zilinsky, Three Hotels,* and *The Paris Letter.* He is a Pulitzer Prize finalist, Drama Desk winner, Humanitas winner, a Guggenheim and an NEA Fellow.

Mr Baitz created the ABC drama *Brothers & Sisters,* has written for *West Wing.* He also adapted his play *The Substance of Fire* for the screen, as well as the screenplay for the Al Pacino movie, *People I Know.* He is currently writing and producing a mini-series for HBO, entitled *Cheney's War,* about the selling of the Iraq Invasion by the Bush administration. He is a founding member of Naked Angels theatre company, and on the faculty of the New School's graduate drama division.

ACKNOWLEDGMENTS

Four Monologues was first produced by Naked Angels at The Space in New York City as a part of *The Naked Truth: Ten Takes on Censorship (& Some Music)* (October 30–November 12, 1990). It was directed by Joe Mantello with the following cast:

Rose Gregorio
Rob Morrow
Geoffrey Nauffts
Lili Taylor

And the following production staff:

Producers	Jenifer Estess, Jack Merrill
Associate Producers	Julianne Hoffenberg, Geoffrey Nauffts, Lili Taylor
Scenic Design	George Xenos
Lighting Design	Brian MacDevitt
Original Music	Jonathan Larson

FOUR MONOLOGUES

Standards & Practices

(A sharp-looking young man is seated in a director's chair, fiddling with his Armani suit.)

They say a lot about the "integrity vacancy" in my profession, which is television. Networks…that's my particular area. Standards and practices.

(Shrugs.)

You find yourself listening to these people. Decent people, but they don't have to face the unwashed masses the way I do in standards and practices. I mean, we're lawyers, you know? I'm no artist.

(Beat.)

I have no pretensions about it. I have to deal with Colgate-Palmolive and Proctor & Gamble and Nestle and General Foods, and these are decent types, these are decent guys. Lawyers, okay, so you get the picture.

(Beat.)

A little dry, maybe, a tendency to look at things as simply as black and white, but after years of having to go through law school, it's not hard to lose your sense of humor.

(Beat.)

But ask yourself this: Who is out there calling the shots? You know? I mean, I really, really despise petty moralizing, I really do.

(Beat.)

And a lot of what I'm asked to do is fatuous even to me, and there is no doubt you could laugh at me—a Jew—smart, you know, you can look at a guy like me and say, "He inherited his liberalism," because I have not lived through anything.

But I'll tell you something, and please, anyone who disagrees with this is—gotta be living in another world…

When you reach the age of about twenty-seven to thirty-two, you basically, you've had to make all the moral choices…

There is nothing you don't have to confront. So listen—I want to ask you this— Who out there is calling the shots? Because let me tell ya', if ya' think it's us guys at standard and practices, I can promise you this: You—are—wrong.

If you think it's the guys at Proctor & Gamble, you—are—wrong.

(Beat.)

Because, basically, what we are, we are men and women who sell certain things. But let me tell you: We get letters, and I mean, they are filled with rage. They are filled with a...a...a passionate anger toward...this coast. This business. What we do. They hate us. So much. Letters from people offended by homosexual acts. AIDS on the Movie of the Week. There are people who are fueled by this.

(*Beat.*)

And I read these letters and I want to take a shower.

(*Beat.*)

People who have this agenda. But they get together, they send these letters to the decent lawyers at Proctor & Gamble, who get scared, and they call me.

(*Beat.*)

We get letters. There is a tide of hatred out there, and you cannot understand it, you cannot fathom the depths. This is a country filled with letter-writers; people who stay up all night, writhing and twisting, people who drive very old cars and have the strangest of habits, and people who have no real control over those habits. This country has a seam of absolute maniacal viciousness, and let me tell you—because you are all really—we're in the same boat—it's you and me against the *treyf* out there—understand this:

They are stronger than us, they outnumber us, and they are angrier than we are; and they do not care about your—your "environment," your "freedom of speech," they want to kill. They want to kill your faggot brother, they want your sister to have that baby, and they—and they—are the people who buy all the shit I sell every night.

(*Beat.*)

I have to make the world smooth for them.

(*Beat.*)

That is my job.

(*Beat. Very quiet:*)

When you hit—you know, age about twenty-eight, you have to make just about every moral decision there is to make.

(*Beat.*)

Like today, Two men kissing?

(*Beat.*)

I had them cut it.

(*Beat.*)

Anything that disturbs the beast out there. No way.

(Beat.)

Just think of me as one of the guardians of your safety; I keep the animals happy. Because they will take over the zoo if we let 'em.

(Picks up the phone.)

Get me Colgate.

Library Lady

(A middle-aged woman at a desk, surrounded by too many books.)

The other day, they had a lecture. Upstairs, in the Oak Room, which was donated by Mrs. Hamilton Straight when we did the renovations and additions fourteen years ago.

I went. I stood there, in the back. An author speaking. An author; they thought, "Let's have culture—after all, this is a library for Cod's sake, a library ought to have a little culture."

And when they asked me, they said, "Hildy, we were thinking, a lecture series for the Oak Room might be nice, what do you think, dear?" This was Arlene Sagitt, from the Board of Education. I said, "Depends on the books, honey, you know?"

(She goes back to her book for a moment, stamps a little rubber library stamp on the front page.)

Three weeks late. It's my biggest problem. I'm the one that gets blamed, I'm the one that gets…well, frankly, I'll say this: There are one or two books that I wouldn't mind if they'd never bring them back. Just keep 'em out forever.

Wouldn't even send them an overdue notice, just quietly look the other way.

Certain books.

They can have 'em, Though I do wonder what they do with them for so long. Do they just keep them on their bedside tables? And pick them up late at night?

And what do they do with these books? I ask myself, What?

(Beat.)

Nobody wants to ask the hard questions, nobody wants to ask these questions, not like when I first came to this library; there were different… book… standards.

(Pause.)

More in keeping with…well, you know what happened yesterday? At the lecture? He read poetry,

Some people, they don't care what they say, they say, "Oh, well, I have thoughts, I have…ideas." I say, keep your ideas to yourself, why don't you? Because that is what people with manners are trained to do, like Nick Carraway at the beginning of *The Great Gatsby* says, "Some people are born with no manners and you just have to forgive them; they haven't had the same advantages as you."

The poet? He said a whole lot. He said a lot. I can tell you.

(She looks down at a piece of paper, looks up, triumphant.)

And I'm not like the biddies, the old wives that volunteer. I'm a withit gal, I think, but I don't know, I have an idea of appropriate and not and—I don't mind repeating the words, the bad words, the four-letter words even, you know, when they start talking about the Lord.

(She smiles, shakes her head.)

So, they think, Oh, someone like— What am I? The housewife in Kansas City? They think someone like me, that I am stupid and pious and have lumpy ankles and a Ph.D in Dewey-Decimal.

(She picks up a book, looks around the room, and stuffs it in her purse.)

So, lately, what I've been doing, I'll tell you, is, I just don't know, maybe it's wrong, but I get rid of them, if they offend me. Because we've been—they make us feel dumb, if we say anything, we get these snickers, intellectual guffaws: "Oh, your values mean nothing."

(Pause.)

We did have a nice lecture about a month ago; a man came from the college to talk about *Paradise Lost.*

(Beat. She smirks.)

My idea, and of course, you know, you get a very thinking crowd, a very… some serious people, and it might not have been the biggest turnout, but people wanted to hear about the fall of man from grace, they wanted to think about their actions.

(She smiles at the audience.)

I have a list.

(Beat.)

This library, it'll be a warm well-lit place, for decent people, who have open minds and charitable hearts. People like you and me.

(She puts another book in her bag after looking around.)

But first I have to get rid of the filth. Don't you agree?

The Girl on the Train

(A young woman in a bulky sweater, her legs tucked under her, sits staring out the window of a train on the New Haven line.)

Just a few days ago, for instance, I was on the train from Meriden, just the other day, the Amtrak, you know, and there was a man.

Much older man, and really thinned out, and I knew he was in trouble, because he was all alone and he had one of those manila envelopes. The kind they put X rays in, and it said "Property of..." some hospital in some little town in Vermont. He kept biting his knuckle, and he was sitting right across from me.

And there was also a lady, much older also, and I carried her bag to the rear car that goes to Alexandria, Virginia, and she needed help. It was too hard to do alone.

A train is a place where you find men and women who like to be helped.

(She smiles, shakes her head, looks down at the floor.)

You don't know what they're like, or who they are, what they do, but they're vulnerable on a train.

And I guess what happens is, it makes you think better of them. That there are decent people in this country. I mean, I say that at home, in New York, and you know it's foolish. I say it at dinner with my boyfriend. He paints... I say, "I think there are decent people here." He smirks. I say, "No really, you know, we're drowning in pesto in this city, we're, I feel like we're just drowning in our smugness and..." And he looks at me. "Are you saying that my art is rarified?" he says.

And I say, "No, no, but we sit around and we make fun of other people's values," He says nothing to this. "There are other values," I say, "certain things mean something to other people and, okay, fine, we want to be left alone to live our lives, but I certainly can understand why a cross marinated in urine might cause anguish, and to make fun of the people who are anguished is to me—narrow-minded and...small."

He says nothing to this.

Actually, he says to me, "Martha, you know what your problem is, your problem is you have a daddy fixation. Like all the Catholic girls from Mineola, you want to do the right thing."

I say nothing.

"Martha," he says, "you're disfiguringly...conventional."

(Pause.)

I've been taking the train a lot lately because Manhattan has gotten so close, you know what I mean? And that decency—that you look for—well, it's always a surprise when you find it in the city.

I do sometimes meet my dad for lunch, and sometimes he says things to me, and I know what he means. He gave me that book by that woman who wrote speeches for the president, and I kept saying to myself, "Yes, she's right." When she said she was offended by the people on the bus with her to Washington in the sixties, because they made fun of the soldiers who were fighting for her, I knew what she meant.

My dad gave me that book.

You know, and he said, he said, "Martha, I think you'll like this, you're a lot like her." Which I'm not.

Sometimes I have dinner with a group of my boyfriend's friends, and we sit at Florent and I just want to—I just want to scream because I feel so—out of touch. "There are other values," I say to them, "besides…I don't know, aesthetics."

I am confused. I know that. I know I am. Please. I— He dragged me to that thing for the guy running against the senator, I mean we all know who I mean, and it was—it was just awful. It was filled with the worst people, and I didn't identify with—

(Beat. She shakes her head. A whisper:)

I just didn't. And I thought, You know, this guy's home state is filled, it's got to be the poorest, the—the most helpless—what do they care about art? Why should they?

(Pause.)

Maybe I like the train because when you're in motion in this country, when you're traveling, you don't have to decide. You can help people with their bags, you can help people get a cup of coffee when they're scared and alone and their X rays— You can watch the rail colors whirr by outside your window in a blur and you don't have to make those decisions.

(Beat.)

And what you believe in.

Broadway

(Dressed in black leather jacket, black jeans, and heavy black boots, a young man stands with his back against a chain link fence, He carries a boom box and is smoking a cigarette.)

Before Kevin died he said to me, "What're you going to do with all those awful old records of mine?" I said, "Well, what do you want me to do, exactly, with *Chorus Line* and *Brigadoon* and, uh, *Carousel,* Kev?"

And he said, "Shit, maybe you should learn 'em all by heart, 'cause you're probably gonna have to do the revivals if you wanna eat."

And we laughed. He was dying; it's really funny how easy it is to laugh when you're dying. He said, "Alex, it's fine that we lost our grant, who needs a militant homo company of dancers in this country?"

I don't have an answer for that. I used to think I did, actually, I mean, I really did. We lost our grant last week, the NEA dropped us, but I don't think it was 'cause we were a homo company, what do you think?

(Beat.)

One by one this company is getting smaller. Paul is a waiter, and he splattered oil from some soft-shell crabs or something and is...looking for another—uh, let's see, you know, six—there are six of us—dead.

(Pause.)

It's hard to dance on AZT.

(Beat, Quiet:)

We had a space a lot like this one, we were friends, just a bunch of us, and why did we dance? I mean, we lost our space, I haven't seen— How many of us are left? After Kevin? Eight.

(Beat.)

We don't even like to see each other, there's nothing left to say, I mean, Jerry was trying to get a job on *Meet Me in St. Louis* and—

(Pause. Quiet:)

Last year—he would not have had to dance for those people, or sing or smile; last year we did not have to pretend to be happy chorus boys. You know? But you start misjudging the world.

(Beat.)

This morning I actually, I sat down and listened to all those musicals of Kevin's, and I'll tell you they were very pleasant, they were just great.

(Beat.)

Fuck it, I threw 'em all out. Maybe the NEA is right. Maybe we were promoting homoeroticism. Yes, sure we were. I thought, Hey, it needs a little promoting, they're still bashin' people's heads in, you know, and—it needs a little promoting; we got guys dragging each other out of the closet and into the tabloids.

(Beat.)

It needs a little promoting, you know. But I misjudged, I really did.

(Beat.)

I said to Kevin, over at Sloan-Kettering, right before he went, I said, "Shit, man, if I'd only known. We should've been promoting *Jerome Robbins' Broadway*. That's where the money is." Kevin laughed. But that's always been my problem: I'm behind the times. Fuck it.

End of Play

BEAUTY RUNS
ON LIGHT FEET
by Kenneth Lonergan

BIOGRAPHY

Kenneth Lonergan has been represented in New York by *Lobby Hero* (Playwrights Horizons, John Houseman Theatre, Drama Desk Best Play Nominee, Outer Critics Circle Best Play and John Gassner Playwrighting Nominee, included in the 2000-2001 Best Plays Annual), *The Waverly Gallery* (Williamstown Theatre Festival, Promenade; 2001 Pulitzer Prize Runner-up), and *This Is Our Youth* (Drama Desk Best Play Nominee). *Lobby Hero* (Olivier Award Nominee for Best Play) and *This Is Out Youth* have also received productions on London's West End. He co-wrote the film *Gangs of New York* which garnered a WGA and Academy Award nomination for Best Original Screenplay. His film *You Can Count On Me,* which he wrote and directed, was nominated for an Academy Award for Best Screenplay, won the Sundance 2000 Grand Jury Prize and The Waldo Salt Screenwriting Award, the NY Film Critics Circle, LA Films Critics Circle, Writers Guild of America and National Board of Review Awards for Best Screenplay of 2001, the AFI Awards for Best Film and Best New Writer, as well as the Sutherland Trophy at the London Film Festival. He is currently in post-production on his film *Margaret,* which he wrote and directed. He is a member of Naked Angels. He is married to actress J. Smith-Cameron.

ACKNOWLEDGMENTS

Beauty Runs On Light Feet was first produced by Naked Angels at The Space in New York City as a part of *The Naked Truth: Ten Takes on Censorship (& Some Music)* (October 30–November 12, 1990). It was directed by Matthew Broderick with the following cast:

MARK REED .... Bruce MacVittie

ELLEN REED.. Lili Taylor

And the following production staff:

Producers... Jenifer Estess, Jack Merrill

Associate Producers.................................... Julianne Hoffenberg,
Geoffrey Nauffts, Lili Taylor

Scenic Design.. George Xenos

Lighting Design .... Brian MacDevitt

CAST OF CHARACTERS

ELLEN REED and MARK REED, a couple in their 30s or 40s with two small children

SETTING

The Reeds' bedroom, in their house in Westchester County, very late at night.

BEAUTY RUNS ON LIGHT FEET

A dark bedroom with a double bed and night table & lamp. ELLEN *is standing in her bathrobe, waiting.*

MARK *comes in. He's wearing a suit, but he's been driving all night.*

He comes in quietly and takes off his jacket. He sits on the edge of the bed. He unlaces and takes off one of his shoes.

ELLEN. Where have you been?

MARK. I went for a drive.

(He take off his other shoe.)

ELLEN. I have had enough of that in my life.

(MARK turns to respond, then thinks better of it. He takes off his socks.)

MARK. Enough of what?

ELLEN. Running out of the house. Screaming and yelling. Screaming and hysteria. I've had enough of that.

MARK. You've had it tough.

(He gets up and starts to go off right, to the bathroom.)

ELLEN. I have *not* had it tough, and you can go f—

(She stops herself. MARK starts to unbutton his shirt.)

MARK. Let's just go to sleep.

ELLEN. Mark, it is two o'clock in the morning.

MARK. Yeah, I know.

ELLEN. What were you doing?

MARK. Just driving.

ELLEN. Where did you drive to?

MARK. Nowhere. I turned around when I got to Hartford. What's the difference? Let's just go to sleep.

ELLEN. *(Lamely hits the pillow.)* I can't sleep...!

(Pause. MARK takes off his shirt and sits on the edge of the bed, in his pants and undershirt.)

MARK. Listen.

(Long pause.)

You just won't see that there's another way of dealing with him besides—

ELLEN. That's *right!* I *don't* see! Because I'm *evil!*

MARK. You're not evil—

ELLEN. I'm *evil* and I'm *destroying* him because I *coddle* him!

MARK. Well honey, you do coddle him.

ELLEN. Right! Because I'm rotten.

MARK. It's got nothing to do with anybody being rotten! It's got to do with not going "Ooh ooh ooh poor Baby!" every time some thing goes wrong! Can't you see the way he feeds into that?! He's nine years old—And he feeds right into that!

ELLEN. No, we should be *tough!* We should punish him because he's *depressed* and he's no *good!* We should be moral-istic and punish him like they did back on the *schtetel!*

ELLEN. Right, because his mother's crazy!

MARK. You're not crazy!

(He knocks over the lamp and she flinches and he walks out. After a moment, she hears him coming back in and she picks up the lamp. He enters, left, grabs a pillow and exits, right, then enters with a blanket and exits left again.)

ELLEN. Oh, you're sleeping in the living room?

MARK. That's right.

ELLEN. Why, because I'm so disgusting?

(He stops, takes a big breath and lets it out.)

ELLEN. Oh don't take a big breath like that!

MARK. Ellen, isn't there any way to discuss this without us getting hysterical?

ELLEN. Oh no, not for me—

MARK. Isn't there any way of discussing this without it being a question of good and evil, and me being moralistic, or whatever you want to say about me—

ELLEN. *(On "Whatever":)* Because you don't hear the tone of your voice.

MARK. I don't know what the tone of my voice is.

ELLEN. That's right, you don't hear it.

MARK. I know I don't hear it and I'm sorry if I don't hear it—

I know, I'm sorry, I'm sorry.

ELLEN. It's that "You didn't do it right, you're no good" tone of voice, and you use the same tone of voice when the kids use too much soap or when they leave the lights on, like

they're criminals because
they forgot to turn the lights
off, Mark!

MARK. Well they can remember to turn the lights off! It's not that hard to remember and it costs money!

ELLEN. See?

MARK. I don't see anything! It costs money and there's no reason they shouldn't learn that, except that if I say anything I can't say ANYTHING! I can't say anything without you jumping in—

ELLEN. Right, right again, it's me!

MARK. Without you jumping in and saying "Don't pay any attention to him, kids, ha ha ha, isn't he cheap, isn't he stingy, oh he's crazy, he's moralistic—"

ELLEN. It's the tone of *voice*.

MARK. And they don't need to use half a bar of soap every time they wash their Goddamn hands!

ELLEN. They're *children!*

MARK. This is stupid, I'm going to bed.

ELLEN. And when Danny comes in the house with that horrible, beaten, miserable face and you sit down and tell me that the thing to do is be good and strict with him, I just want to vomit.

MARK. I'm going to bed.

(He exits, left. Pause. She looks through the stuff on the night table and finds a cigarette which she lights. She gets up and goes to the door, left.)

ELLEN. Mark.

(Silence.)

Mark.

MARK. *(Off:)* What.

ELLEN. I don't want the children to see you sleeping in the living room.

MARK. *(Off:)* It's fine.

ELLEN. I don't want that. Come back to bed.

MARK. *(Off:)* I don't want to.

(Pause.)

ELLEN. Mark, I really don't want the children to wake up and find you sleeping in the living room—

MARK. *(Off:)* OK OK OK!

ELLEN. *(Without stopping:)* —because *you* don't have to deal with them all day long when they ask were we fighting, what's the matter, is Daddy leaving again—

MARK. *(Entering:)* OK! OK!

ELLEN. I just don't want that.

> (MARK *gets in bed with his pillow.* ELLEN *waves away some of the cigarette smoke.)*

ELLEN. Sorry about the smoke. I'll open the window.

MARK. Forget about it.

> (ELLEN *puts out the cigarette.)*

ELLEN. Three more weeks until I quit.

> *(Silence.)*

MARK. Can I turn the light off?

> (ELLEN *does not respond.)*

Maybe we can take him to a psychiatrist…

ELLEN. I don't want that.

MARK. We could try giving him something like a structure of some kind that he had to work with, so that when he doesn't know what to—

> (ELLEN *sighs loudly.)*

—to do with himself, he has some things he knows he *has* to do. I don't think that's the same as putting him in a concentration camp.

> (ELLEN *doesn't respond. Silence.)*

You know, there's not one person in this whole house who I haven't wanted to kill, at one time or another.

ELLEN. That's a charming thing to say.

> *(Pause.)*

MARK. You tell me I'm too strict…

ELLEN. Let's just drop it.

MARK. No, I just want to say this one thing! And then we'll forget about it and we'll do it your way. Which is the way we end up doing it anyway, so at least I can have my say without everybody getting hysterical.

> (ELLEN *does not respond. He sits up.)*

MARK. Ok?

ELLEN. Sure. Say whatever you want.

> (MARK *gets up and walks around.)*

MARK. I was going to say, Ellen, that you say I'm too strict, and I'm so mean, and I never let the kids have any fun…but *you* don't… Never mind that. But do you remember the time when we got the new sofa and the kids were jumping all over it? They were playing some kind of crazy kamikaze game, and with my usual tact I screamed at them and I told them to get the hell off the sofa? Do you remember that?

(ELLEN does not respond.)

I said do you *remember* that?

ELLEN. *(On "do":)* Yes, yes, I remember that. I'm sure this is all leading to some profound moral lesson on the iniquity of lax discipline.

MARK. Can I PLEASE finish my sentence before you start that stuff! PLEASE PLEASE PLEASE! I'm begging you, stop talking in that infantile sarcastic way!

ELLEN. Oh I'm sorry if it's not as sophisticated as *your* sarcasm—

MARK. *(Falling to his knees:)* PLEASE! I'M BEGGING YOU!

(Silence.)

This is not a story about how evil you are. Or anything moral at all. You said in front of the kids that I was being moralistic, from the schtetel, like Grampa— as you frequently do. And usually it's funny. And you told me how crazy I was being and what's *wrong* with me, and why shouldn't they play on the sofa, et cetera et cetera, and so naturally, the minute I left the room they both started bouncing up and down on the sofa. So the sofa is ruined now, by the way, eight hundred dollar sofa, but never mind *that.* But you seem to— ...Well, there's no way to say this without you thinking I'm accusing you of something.

ELLEN. What?

MARK. No. Forget it.

ELLEN. What?

MARK. Well, two days later, Danny is jumping up and down on the sofa, and he takes a jump, and he overshot the sofa. He jumped too far and fell over the arm head-first onto the floor and he smashed his head.

ELLEN. Oh for God's sake...

MARK. Yes, you can *say* "For God's sake," but I saw this happen and my *heart* stopped beating. And I ran over to him and on the way over I'm already imagining him in the emergency room with the orthopedic surgeon standing there telling me, "I'm sorry, Dr. Reed, but his neck is broken—" and by the time I got there, obviously he was fine, he was crying, he was mad at the sofa— But I *blind* with rage. *Blind.* Because he could have been seriously hurt—

ELLEN. Mark: sweetheart: children get into accidents.

MARK. I *know* that, but it's like anything out of my mouth is dismissed without you even thinking about it. It's either an accusation or a moralistic tirade, and then once in a while it turns out I don't know what I'm talking about— I mean, once in a while it turns out I do know what I'm talking about—

(They both laugh.)

MARK. *(Making a joke:)* You know, *once* in a while I'm wrong... *(Pause.)* But you do do that, honey, you really do, and I might be right once in a while.

ELLEN. I'm going to sleep.

MARK. OK. OK. Me too.

(He gets into bed. She shuts out the light.)

Maybe *we* should see a psychiatrist.

ELLEN. No, you mean I should see a psychiatrist.

MARK. Let's forget about it.

(They lie there for a second.)

There is no way to find out the right thing to do if you can't have a conversation about it.

ELLEN. You don't know how to have a conversation.

MARK. Well, I thought I was—

ELLEN. All you know how to do is find a culprit.

(Pause.)

MARK. Well then let's forget about the whole fuckin' thing.

(He turns away from her. Fade out.)

End of Play

SEX WITH THE CENSOR
by Theresa Rebeck

BIOGRAPHY

Theresa Rebeck is a widely produced playwright throughout the United States and abroad. Past New York productions of her work include *Mauritius* at the Biltmore Theatre in a Manhattan Theater Club Production; *The Scene, The Water's Edge, Loose Knit, The Family of Mann* and *Spike Heels* at Second Stage; *Bad Dates, The Butterfly Collection* and *Our House* at Playwrights Horizons; and *View of the Dome* at New York Theatre Workshop. *Omnium Gatherum* (co-written, finalist for the Pulitzer Prize in 2003) was featured at the Humana Festival, and had a commercial run at the Variety Arts Theatre. Her newest work, *The Understudy,* will open in New York at the Laura Pels Theater at the Roundabout in the Fall of 2009.

All of Ms. Rebeck's past produced plays are published by Smith and Kraus as *Theresa Rebeck: Complete Plays, Volumes I, II* and *III* and in acting editions available from Samuel French. Ms. Rebeck's other publications are *Free Fire Zone,* a book of comedic essays about writing and show business. She has written for *American Theatre Magazine* and has had excerpts of her plays published in the *Harvard Review.* Ms. Rebeck's first novel, *Three Girls and Their Brother,* was published by Random House/Shaye Areheart Books and is available online and at fine booksellers everywhere.

In television, Ms. Rebeck has written for *Dream On, Brooklyn Bridge, L.A. Law, American Dreamer, Maximum Bob, First Wave,* and *Third Watch.* She has been a writer/producer for *Canterbury's Law, Smith, Law and Order: Criminal Intent* and *NYPD Blue.* Her produced feature films include *Harriet the Spy, Gossip,* and the independent feature *Sunday on the Rocks.* Awards include the Mystery Writer's of America's Edgar Award, the Writer's Guild of America award for Episodic Drama, the Hispanic Images Imagen Award, and the Peabody, all for her work on NYPD Blue. She has won the National Theatre Conference Award (for *The Family of Mann*), and was awarded the William Inge New Voices Playwriting Award in 2003 for *The Bells. Mauritius* was originally produced at Boston's Huntington Theatre, where it received the 2007 IRNE Award for Best New Play as well as the Eliot Norton Award.

Ms. Rebeck is originally from Cincinnati and holds an MFA in Playwriting and a PhD. in Victorian Melodrama, both from Brandeis University. She is a proud board member of the Dramatists Guild and has taught at Brandeis University and Columbia University. She lives in Brooklyn with her husband Jess Lynn and two children, Cooper and Cleo.

ACKNOWLEDGMENTS

Sex with the Censor was first produced by Naked Angels at The Space in New York City as a part of *The Naked Truth: Ten Takes on Censorship (& Some Music)* (October 30–November 12, 1990). It was directed by Jace Alexander with the following cast:

WOMAN	Lisa Beth Miller
MAN	Billy Strong

And the following production staff:

Producers	Jenifer Estess and Jack Merrill
Associate Producers	Julianne Hoffenberg, Geoffrey Nauffts, Lili Taylor
Scenic Design	George Xenos
Lighting Design	Brian MacDevitt
Original Music	Jonathan Larson

CAST OF CHARACTERS

WOMAN, a prostitute

MAN, the censor

SETTING

A bare room. A small cot covered with a bedspread has been set to one side. There is also a chair.

SEX WITH THE CENSOR

Lights up. A provocatively dressed WOMAN *sits on the bed. A* MAN *stands across the room, by the chair. He wears a suit.*

WOMAN. So, how do you like it? Sitting, standing, or are you a traditional kind of guy?

MAN. What?

WOMAN. Tell you what; we'll improvise. *(She stands and crosses to him.)* Just see what happens, huh?

(She reaches for his jacket, as if to take it off him. He backs away from her.)

MAN. Don't do that.

WOMAN. Oh. Sorry. Some guys…

MAN. I don't want you to do that.

WOMAN. Whatever. *(She turns and takes off her skirt. Underneath she wears black stockings and panties.)* No shit, most guys like, you know, to be undressed. I think it reminds them of their mother, although I don't know why you'd want to be thinking about your mother at a time like this. I mean, I know about the whole psychology thing, Oedipus, whatever—we do, we talk about that stuff—but I have to say I never believed most of it. That guys want to fuck their mothers. That just, frankly, that makes no sense to me. I mean, if it's true, you guys are even crazier than I thought, you know what I mean? I mean, no offense or anything.

MAN. Stop talking.

WOMAN. *(Unbuttoning her blouse:)* Oh, sorry. I know, I kind of run on. Especially late in the day; I get tired and anything that comes into my head comes right out of my mouth. I don't know. A lot of guys like it, which is lucky for me because I just, I don't even really know when it's happening—

MAN. Don't do that.

WOMAN. Excuse me?

MAN. Don't take your shirt off.

WOMAN. Oh. Okay. *(She starts to button up again.)*

MAN. No. Leave it like that. I want to see that I can't see.

WOMAN. What?

MAN. If you button it, I can't see. I want to see that I can't see.

WOMAN. Oh. Sure.

(She stands for a moment, in the unbuttoned shirt and stockings. He stares at her. He is fully dressed.)

33

WOMAN. So…are we ready to get going here? I mean, I don't mean to rush things, but it's been my experience that it kind of helps to hit the ground running, you know, just let her rip, and since you're not particularly interested in small talk, we probably should just get to it, huh? *(Pause.)* So are we, what? You need a hand with this clothes thing here?

MAN. No.

WOMAN. No.

> *(Pause. They stare at each other.)*

WOMAN. Okay, sure, you're shy. I'm sensitive to that. We'll just take this real slow. *(She reaches for his jacket carefully.)*

MAN. Don't touch me.

WOMAN. Honey, that's not going to be entirely possible under the circumstances here—

> *(She tries to take the jacket off him. He shoves her, hard.)*

WOMAN. Hey, don't get rough with me, asshole. That's not the deal, all right?

MAN. I told you. I don't want you to touch me. We don't do that.

WOMAN. Well, what do we do?

> *(He looks at her. He pulls the chair over, back to the audience. He sits in it.)*

MAN. Stand here.

> *(He points in front of him. She crosses warily and faces him. His back is to the audience.)*

WOMAN. *(Irritated:)* So, what, you just want to look, is that it? Fine. Whatever. But it's the same price, okay? We're not sailing into discount land because you're in some sort of fucking mood here, okay?

MAN. Don't say that.

WOMAN. I'm just telling you the rules.

MAN. No, I tell you the rules.

WOMAN. Listen—

MAN. I don't want you to use that word. You've used it twice. I don't want to hear that word.

WOMAN. What word?

MAN. You know the word.

WOMAN. What word? You mean fuck?

MAN. I don't want to hear it.

WOMAN. Sorry. I mean, I just, I thought that's what we were here for.

MAN. I DON'T WANT TO HEAR IT.

WOMAN. Okay, fine, I won't say anything. I'll just stand here. You can pay me to stand here; that's fine by me. Fucking weirdo. Sorry.

(He sits, staring. Pause.)

MAN. Tell me what you want.

WOMAN. Tell you what I—you want me to tell you what I want?

MAN. Yes.

WOMAN. Okay. I want to wrap this up and go home and see my kid. It's been a long day—

MAN. No.

WOMAN. No.

MAN. No.

WOMAN. That's not what I want.

MAN. No.

WOMAN. Okay, then you tell me what I do want because I mean, I am in the dark here, all right? Usually, I have to say, usually there is not a lot of confusion about how to proceed, but—

MAN. Stop talking.

WOMAN. Stop talking. Right. I forgot.

MAN. Tell me what you want.

(Pause. She looks at him.)

WOMAN. *(Matter of fact:)* Okay. Let's try this. I want you.

MAN. Yes.

WOMAN. Yes. That's a yes. Here we go. I want you…inside of me.

MAN. Yes.

WOMAN. Two yeses. This is a trend. I want to suck your cock.

MAN. No.

WOMAN. No. That's not what I want. Okay, fine, I—fuck, I don't know what the fuck—

MAN. NO.

WOMAN. No, sorry, I didn't mean to use that word, I meant, I mean, I meant DARN. Darn.

MAN. Yes.

WOMAN. Yes. Darn. Sorry. I'm a little slow, darn it. *(Pause.)* I want you… in my mouth?

(He does not respond.)

WOMAN. I want…to touch you.

MAN. *(Quiet:)* No.

WOMAN. But I can't.

MAN. Yes.

WOMAN. I want you to look at me...and not see me.

MAN. Yes.

WOMAN. Yes. I want to stand in front of you naked, with clothes on.

MAN. Yes.

WOMAN. I get this. You want to have sex without sex.

MAN. *(Aroused:)* Yes. Tell me what you want.

> *(Pause. The WOMAN stares at him for a long moment, then turns and picks up her shoes.)*

WOMAN. No. I won't do it. This is sick, this is really—

MAN. Do you want the money or not?

> *(Pause.)*

WOMAN. Yeah. I want the money.

MAN. Then tell me what you want.

> *(Pause. The WOMAN sets her shoes down, turns and looks at him.)*

WOMAN. I want...I want you in me outside of me.

MAN. Yes.

WOMAN. I want you to touch me...without feeling me. I want words with no voice. Sex with no heart. Love without bones.

MAN. *(Overlap:)* Yes. Yes.

WOMAN. *(Overlap:)* Skin without skin. I want blind eyes.

MAN. Yes.

WOMAN. I want you to stare me dead. I want you to lick me dry. I want you to take my words. Wipe me clean. Make me nothing. Let me be nothing for you. Let me be nothing. Let me be nothing.

MAN. *(Overlap:)* Yes. Yes. Yes!

> *(He comes without touching himself. She watches him, dispassionate. There is a long pause. They stare at each other.)*

MAN. You disgust me.

WOMAN. Yeah. I know. That'll be $200. Sir.

> *(Blackout.)*

End of Play

Josh Malina and Xander Berkley in *Snuff*
Naked Angels at The Coast in Los Angeles (1994).

SNUFF
by Frank Pugliese

BIOGRAPHY

Some of Frank Pugliese's credits for the stage include: *Kaos* (New York Theatre Workshop); *Aven'U Boys* (Off-B'way, Obie Award); *The King of Connecticut, The Talk, The Alarm* (all with Naked Angels); *Hope is the Thing with Feathers, Late Night—Early Morning* (The Drama Dept.); *The Crazy Girl* (NY Stage and Film, Gloucester Stage). His film credits include: *Born to Run* (Fox); *Infamous* (Hart-Sharp, HBO); *Shot in the Heart* (directed by Agineszka Holland, produced by Barry Levinson and Tom Fontana). His television credits include: "Night of the Living Dead," *Homicide* (WGA Award); "Love and Blood," *Fallen Angels* (Cable Ace Award Nomination).

Mr. Pugliese has directed numerous Off-Broadway productions and is a former Artistic Director of Naked Angels. He won the Forbes Herman award for playwriting. He was honored by New York University's Tisch School of the Arts as their outstanding alumni in the field. Mr. Pugliese is a consultant for the Cherry Lane Mentor Program. He teaches playwriting and screenwriting at Columbia University and the New School. He is a proud member of Naked Angels and the Drama Dept.

ACKNOWLEDGMENTS

Snuff was first produced by Naked Angels at The Space in New York City as a part of *The Naked Truth: Ten Takes on Censorship (& Some Music)* (October 30–November 12, 1990). It was directed by Harold Guskin with the following cast:

SID	Bruce MacVittie
FRED	Fisher Stevens

And the following production staff:

Producers	Jenifer Estess, Jack Merrill
Associate Producers	Julianne Hoffenberg, Geoffrey Nauffts, Lili Taylor
Scenic Design	George Xenos
Lighting Design	Brian MacDevitt
Original Music	Jonathan Larson

CAST OF CHARACTERS

SID

FRED

PRODUCTION NOTE

In a Naked Angels production of the play several years after the initial one, the reference to "Nicaragua" was changed to "formerly Yugoslavia."

And "the Sandinistas" was changed to "a Serbian."

And "this guy's a Contra..." was changed to "this guy was in the military..."

And "Indian girl" was changed to "Muslim girl."

The choice is at the discretion of subsequent productions.

SNUFF

An editing room. SID *and* FRED.

SID. Save the head comin' off for later.

FRED. I thought we'd end with the flag.

SID. Are you wealthy?

FRED. No. Why?

SID. 'Cause only wealthy people care about art.

FRED. It's symbolism, not art.

SID. The head comin' off is definitely the climax.

FRED. And the blood shot?

SID. Show the head rollin' a little. And then the blood sprayin' in slow motion... Freeze, with the stain on the wall. You notice how the stain looks like a skull. Then, boom, cut to the hospital.

FRED. And the nurse?

SID. Don't get ahead of yourself.

FRED. I like to see the whole thing.

SID. Well keep your head on... Head! Get it!

FRED. Yeah...

SID. You have to have sense of humor about this business.

FRED. We could do a nice thing with the sex scene.

SID. Hey, hey, hey, this ain't in black and white.

FRED. I shoulda never ran it for you.

SID. *(Laughing:)* Ain't no guy in a black turtleneck goin' around sayin' communist.

FRED. Community, he says community!

SID. Those horny little NYU girls who go to sleep with books between their legs must love this shit.

FRED. I just got a great idea for the sex, that's all.

SID. I like sex as much as the next guy, but Romy says we're in we're out... Well you know what I mean.

FRED. Why?

SID. He doesn't want an X or whatever they're gonna call it. He wants the ones under seventeen.

FRED. We don't have to show it goin' in or anything...

SID. That guy's on so many steroids he can't even find it.

FRED. I thought the whole thing was him makin' love in the hospital bed with bombs droppin' around'em.

SID. If it gets an X, nobody's gonna see it except some pervert in the front row jerkin' off inta his baseball hat... You don't get word of mouth from a jerk-off... I tell you that from experience.

FRED. Whatta you mean?

SID. Whatta you mean?

FRED. I, I mean, howda we cut it.

SID. Look we got this guy killin' Arabs for the whole fuckin' movie, right. Then we hav'em fuck an Arab. Forget that he's got a bullet in'em and he's sewed up and probably couldn't get it up for Miss America...it's confusing. Keep it simple. The brown guys are bad. The white guys are good.

FRED. WE got a lot dead brown guys.

SID. People like dead brown guys. It gets their mind off their troubles.

FRED. But what happens to her character?

SID. Character? What are you, professor "I teach film 'cause I can't make one"?

FRED. What about her?

SID. She kisses him, but she's an Arab, see? He looks into her beautiful Persian eyes, but he don't trust her, he don't know. We got that piece of film where he doesn't know, that look he does of "I don't know." Boom! The hospital blows. WE cut to the arm flyin' outta the window. I love that arm.

FRED. But Sid, the whole thing was, he fucks her, she tells him about the bomb 'cause her brother's with the Arabs...

SID. Too fuckin' complicated. We should stick to the action. These fuckin' writers need a reason for everything.

FRED. What, the hosptical gets leveled and he walks out?

SID. Yeah.

FRED. What is he, Superman?

SID. He's American... Think of it. All these Arabs go up like a puff of black smoke. And through the smoke he walks out, without a scratch. The audience is going to eat it like popcorn.

FRED. I don't know... It's a whole subplot.

SID. You worry about subplot when you were cuttin' porn?

FRED. No...

SID. I wonder why he's licking her asshole. Oh, look, he's fuckin' her up the ass, does that further the subplot?

FRED. This is my first studio picture.

SID. You make a lot of money doin' porn.

FRED. Enough.

SID. It's film-making.

FRED. Made some good money on one job. Some shooter from down south. He got all mixed up that the Moral Majority was gonna drop a suit on him like a stack of bibles.

SID. For how much?

FRED. Don't matter who wins. The legal fees close you down anyways. You do anything down there a little off the main road, they sue you.

SID. So, the job...

FRED. So, he's got me cuttin' his film from hard to soft. You know. Twelve hours a day, I'm pullin' out close-ups—penis, vagina, penis, vagina...

SID. You musta went nuts.

FRED. I went numb... The joke is, I take the clips and cut'em together. I'm takin' only close-ups of fuckin', right? Put some punk music in the background —I won a film festival in Berlin. Thousand dollars.

SID. And it's on TV too.

FRED. Like a soap or somethin'?

SID. Nah, I come home, I see my kid... He's watchin' this shit off the satellite. I don't know where it's comin' from—France or somethin'... I'm like, "Change the channel, watch something good like a cop show or some- thin'."

FRED. So whatta you do?

SID. Nah, you teach the kid what to watch. Sex is bad. Cops are good.

FRED. Shit, what about the flag?

SID. What about it?

FRED. Watch!

SID. I see what you're sayin'.

FRED. I mean does Romy want the bullets goin' through the flag?

SID. Fuck!

FRED. The Arab, he takes the flag, and he wraps it around himself like a tunic, right? Then we cut to bonehead and his M.K.

SID. Cut to the Arab smilin'.

FRED. Right.

SID. See, the Arab is thinkin' he's not gonna shoot me with an American flag wrapped around me.

FRED. He turns him into Swiss cheese.

SID. Yeah.

FRED. And look at the flag, it's laid out in the desert full of holes. Does Romy want that?

SID. You know somethin'...

(Pause.)

You're good. You're really good.

FRED. Somehow, if the head comin' off belongs to the Arab in the flag.

SID. Boom! Beautiful.

FRED. Long shots.

SID. They all look alike, right?

(Laughs.)

FRED. Bloody.

SID. This is my third picture with Romy. Romy Halestorm turns blood into art... Does blood bother you?

FRED. Excuse me?

SID. Romy loves red.

FRED. I'm not havin' nightmares or anything, if that's what you mean.

SID. Good, 'cause violence is normal. That's why it's scary. Violence happens every day. Sex on the other hand, if you're lucky—

FRED. I like a little sex in a movie.

SID. Like in the old days. How'd you meet Romy?

FRED. At the Berlin festival. He called my movie a symphony.

SID. Romy knows what people want... They're all locked up behind bars and burglar alarms and pit bulls and forty-fives. They sit in front of the TV all night watching a murder in Minnesota, a rape in Houston, a robbery in New York. They watch those shows. 911, real cops, the murder of the week. They get nuts. So a movie where some bad guys get blown away... It's a release.

FRED. Who's to say what art is, right?

SID. When we wrap, we'll go to Times Square. Not some Hollywood premiere... There, they scream at the screen. These people applaud a good killing. They watch the way the blood shoots off a body. These people are educated in violence.

FRED. I don't know if that's the kind of audience I want to be a part of.

SID. Whatta you mean?

FRED. It's just scary.

SID. This movie is gonna make big money.

FRED. It's a big break for me.

SID. You're gonna get into the union.

FRED. I know.

SID. You like this job?

FRED. What's not to like?

SID. You think this is obscene?

FRED. No.

SID. You're a professional.

FRED. I am.

SID. I'll tell you what's obscene. A lot of art. Not just movies. But I understand. If we're gonna give tax money to artists. Sure, there's shit you're not gonna like... Right?

FRED. Right.

SID. This whole censorship thing is bullshit.

FRED. I been so busy on the film...

SID. You wanna know what's really obscene? The S and L is obscene. Censorship is one big fuckin' distraction. These fuckin' politicians are worse than any whore on film. They stand up there, yeah we ripped you off for thousands but if you re-elect me I'll never give another dollar to a homo with a camera. You got money?

FRED. Some.

SID. 'Cause the only law in this country is money.

FRED. I think it's a question of responsibility.

SID. That's right. Take your money out of the bank. Do you know the FDIC has only sixty cents for every hundred of your dollars? Do you know that for the first time since 1933 banks are allowed to invest in stocks. So while everybody is playin' the violin for censorship, the kingdom is burning down. NO, who's responsible?

FRED. Where do I put it?

SID. You wanna double it, maybe triple, maybe ten times?

FRED. Sure.

SID. You ever seen a snuff?

FRED. A real one?

SID. No, a fake one.

FRED. At a producer's party once.

SID. So you know?

FRED. Well, I didn't look at it, really.

SID. There's a whole underground. Guys who pay top dollar for this stuff. Rich guys, successful. Suit and ties and shit… Are you married?

FRED. Gettin'…

SID. You love her.

FRED. I guess, yeah.

SID. Good. So you could use the money.

FRED. I need money.

SID. A lot of them are prostitutes and junkies.

FRED. And they don't know, right?

SID. You went to college. If they knew, would they do it?

FRED. What if they're kidnapped or somethin'?

SID. Well, this is not like that. Romy and me made some friends while were shootin' in the desert.

FRED. Arabs?

SID. Nah, American. We met a missionary. And I don't mean religion. Oh man, this guy would make a movie. He kills for money… In the desert, the guy's a fuckin' real-life Rambo. Ex-Green Beret, C.I.A., Secret Service and who the fuck knows what else. —I mean mercenary. Anyways, he's got, or knows about, some film… The weekend, we meet in Jerusalem. The Holy City. In the middle of all this hell on earth. We meet this guy, I'm tellin' you, suit, he looks like somebody shakin' hands with the president on TV. So we talk. All-American type. President of his fraternity. I mean you look at this guy and you think he's a fuckin' yuppie. Oh, he was an actor too. Real good lookin'. He's in the third reel… But, he's just a go-between. He brings us up the elevator, ritzy hotel, marble and brass, right? And in the room is this fat fuck from Nicaragua.

FRED. Like the Sandinistas.

SID. But this guy's a Contra… You see, he got his hands on some dead cameraman's gun.

FRED. A real gun?

SID. Nah, the camera… I don't remember what network. Anyways they raped and tortured this Indian girl. Sixteen, maybe seventeen. And they want to sell the footage.

FRED. How much money?

SID. They need money, a lot of money, they're like doin' shit in Sarajevo and other holes down there, so they need the money. Do you wanna make money?

FRED. Holy shit.

SID. Lemme tell you somethin', if those countries turn down there, and they don't pay back their loans, our banks are goin' under...

FRED. I'm talkin' about the girl.

SID. But there's the beauty, when Romy sells it, we get paid in Deutschmarks. Solid money, not like dollars.

    *(*SID *starts to put the reels on the machine.)*

FRED. Sid!

SID. You wanna see the footage?

FRED. I don't think this is right.

SID. Just look at the footage... Freddy, you, me and Romy, we could be working together for a long time.

FRED. This is fake. That isn't real.

SID. I hope it's real, that's what people pay for. No FX could do this.

FRED. I'm a filmmaker.

SID. So, film is film. We cut the film, not the people. We're professionals... Look at the footage.

FRED. I don't wanna look.

SID. Just look if you wanna look.

    (Pause.)

    *(*FRED *looks at the film.)*

You looked!

    *(*FRED *covers his mouth.)*

    (Blackout.)

End of Play

naked
rights

COQ AU VIN
by Jon Robin Baitz

BIOGRAPHY

Jon Robin Baitz is the author of a number of plays including *The Substance of Fire, A Fair Country, Ten Unknowns, Mizlansky/Zilinsky, Three Hotels,* and *The Paris Letter.* He is a Pulitzer Prize finalist, Drama Desk winner, Humanitas winner, a Guggenheim and an NEA Fellow.

Mr Baitz created the ABC drama *Brothers & Sisters,* has written for *West Wing.* He also adapted his play *The Substance of Fire* for the screen, as well as the screenplay for the Al Pacino movie, *People I Know.* He is currently writing and producing a mini-series for HBO, entitled *Cheney's War,* about the selling of the Iraq Invasion by the Bush administration. He is a founding member of Naked Angels theatre company, and on the faculty of the New School's graduate drama division.

ACKNOWLEDGMENTS

Coq Au Vin was first produced by Naked Angels at The Space in New York City as a part of *Naked Rights* (December 6–21, 1991). It was directed by Joe Mantello with the following cast:

CHICKEN ONE	Patrick Breen
CHICKEN TWO	Bradley White
MAN	Garreth Williams

And the following production staff:

Co-Directors	Jace Alexander, Paul S. Eckstein
Producer	Jenifer Estess
Coordinating Producer	Julianne Hoffenberg
Scenic Design	George Xenos
Lighting Design	Brian MacDevitt
Costume Design	Rosi Zingales
Sound Design	Guy Sherman, Aural Fixation

CAST OF CHARACTERS

CHICKEN ONE
CHICKEN TWO
MAN

COQ AU VIN

Lights come up on two people in chicken suits, center stage.

CHICKEN ONE. Cunts. Cheap, miserable, brassy, lowdown, good-for-nothing, sadistic, cheating cunts.

CHICKEN TWO. Please don't cause a scene. I beg of you.

(CHICKEN TWO does a little chicken dance.)

CHICKEN ONE. *(Sotta voce, scornful:)* We're supposed to be happy. Happy. Hah! Look at you.

(CHICKEN TWO does nothing—except try to look dignified.)

You're beneath contempt. Not even to protest. Not to raise your voice like I have. To sit silently and let it happen to you, it's disgusting.

CHICKEN TWO. Look who's talking, pal.

CHICKEN ONE. And what exactly is that supposed to mean?

CHICKEN TWO. Quiet! They'll catch us! Then where'll we be? Then what?

(They make little pecking motions and chicken noises.)

I'm just happy to participate.

CHICKEN ONE. *(Mimics in a pansy voice:)* I'm just happy to par-tic-ipate! God, you make me sick to my stomach. To think that you talked me into this.

CHICKEN TWO. Yeah, you and your busy schedule. You! You haven't worked in a year and a half.

CHICKEN ONE. That's right, I haven't. That's precisely correct. Exactly. And why have I not worked? In a year and a half?

(Beat.)

CHICKEN TWO. I don't care to discuss it.

CHICKEN ONE. That is what they've done to us. Reduced us to chickens at the County Fair. Yes. You know, I mean, I have to actually laugh because no training, you know, not the Royal Academy or Strasberg or that bitch Adler could have ever, ever prepared me for this: Reduced to a barnyard animal at a pageant. A chicken suit.

CHICKEN TWO. I'm just glad to be alive! What about that? You have no survival mechanism! You think the world is safe? Doesn't this prove that it isn't? That an actor of your caliber is reduced to playing a chicken? You think there's respect? You think they—you actually believed that because you had talent they'd spare you!

(They make chicken noises—clucks and pecks.)

CHICKEN ONE. I'm at the point where I'd rather die. You're right; I never did *Hamlet.* I never did *Enemy of the People,* I never did Lorca, Marlowe, I never did any of it. No, I never did it. Right. *(Beat.)* Oh, it's fine to be a fucking chicken, could've been worse, they might've offered me the part of the—

CHICKEN TWO. *(Cuts him off impatiently:)* At least you get unemployment benefits because of this job! You won't starve!

CHICKEN ONE. *(Agonized, heartbroken:)* What good does that do me now? I have no self-respect!

CHICKEN TWO. *(Trying not to panic:)* If you continue to yell, Michael, then the stage manager will alert the director and someone will come and then something...*awful* will happen. Just *awful.* Look at the bright side. Connect to the...chicken inside of you. Think of it as an exercise.

(They cluck and bock.)

CHICKEN ONE. I can't stand this ignominy any longer! I simply won't tolerate it!

CHICKEN TWO. *(Holds* CHICKEN ONE *to the ground.)* Jesus Michael I beg of you don't get us killed! Please. Please. *(Holds his hand over* MICHAEL's *mouth—or beak.)* Please why can't you be far-sighted? Think of a day when this'll be a laugh? There are people here who have to play pigs, they're lying in pig shit, for ten days! The chicken is a good job. It's a *sign* from them that we'll be rehabilitated. Chicken is harmless. A coward. Let them. Let them think we're cowards. I love you. I don't care that they have reduced us to this, I don't care about the theatre we wanted, I care about you! I love you.

CHICKEN ONE. *(After a moment.)* Look at us. Two bent chickens at a country fair. There is nothing comic about it. Nothing.

CHICKEN TWO. Look. At least people are laughing. That's something.

CHICKEN ONE. They're laughing, you prick, because they're watching a grown man, an *actor,* in a chicken suit, a *molting* chicken suit for God's sake, hop about in a fucking *coop!* I'd laugh too if it wasn't me!

CHICKEN TWO. No, Michael, they're laughing because they appreciate our essaying of a chicken; they laugh because they are delighted.

CHICKEN ONE. Are you fuckin' nuts? Are you kiddin' me? What do you think you *are?* This audience? This is Ice Capades! This is Holiday on Ice! This is your audience! They're laughing because they smell your humiliation, you positively reek of it! "Essaying of a chicken." Please! Don't... make...me laugh!

(Pause. CHICKEN TWO *hops away.)*

CHICKEN TWO. Why can't I be allowed to believe in myself?

CHICKEN ONE. What do you think? You think you're making a statement? You think you're saying something? What exactly do you think you're saying to them?

CHICKEN TWO. *(Calm, noble:)* If...they are aware of who we are, actors, we have been brought...low, and yet, who can endow this chore with some semblance of seriousness—some—you know—sense of...pride—then they know we have not been destroyed, they know we are not complicit. There.

CHICKEN ONE. If you believe that horseshit, you're an asshole.

CHICKEN TWO. *(Simple, direct. Straight:)* Michael. Why are you so mean to me?

CHICKEN ONE. Oh, come on.

CHICKEN TWO. No, I mean, this'll be over soon. All of it. You know? Can't you find it in you to be a little bit solicitous, you know, tender? I mean, fuck, I feel bad too. You think I don't know I'm lying to myself? My parents sent me to acting school. My parents came to my plays. My parents loved me, they never dreamt of this kind of treatment for me, and they—they knew everything about me—every boy I—they didn't care—they loved me, they taught me love. And I love you, and I won't be made to feel silly or ridiculous just because I've been forced to wear a fucking chicken suit and humiliate myself for some rubes. This is not humiliation. Humiliation is forgetting how to love, how to love... I'd rather die than that...and they can put me in a turtle suit, Michael, and shit on me and laugh at me because I amuse them as a queer pansy or a lefty or whore or a hooker or whatever they say, but Michael, you know, it's only a suit. It's only a suit. It's only a suit.

(MICHAEL says nothing. They bock.)

MICHAEL. I love you too, Terry. I love you too.

(A man walks onstage. He carries a pointer.)

MAN. These are chickens. They make up a large part of the barnyard world, and they give us eggs, and we eat them and they provide a source of protein for all. The chicken, my friends, she is a truly multifaceted addition to our world. *(Takes out a knife and quickly cuts TERRY's throat.)* And a friend to mankind at the Nation's table. *(Exits.)*

MICHAEL. Bock-bock. Cheep-cheep.

(He holds the dying TERRY in his arms as lights fade down.)

End of Play

PAY-PER-KILL
by Warren Leight

BIOGRAPHY

Warren Leight's *Side Man* won the 1999 Tony Award for Best Play. His other plays include *No Foreigners Beyond This Point* (Baltimore Center Stage premiere); *James and Annie* (Ensemble Theatre of Cincinnati premiere); *Glimmer, Glimmer and Shine* (ATCA Nomination); *Mayor, the Musical* (Drama Desk Nomination); *Fame Takes a Holiday* (co-written); *Stray Cats;* and *The Loop.* Recent publications: *Dark No Sugar,* a collection of one acts; *Leading Women: Plays for Actresses II;* DPS's *Outstanding Men's Monologues 2001- 2002;* Ensemble Studio Theatre's Marathon 2000 collection; and *Dramatics* magazine. Screenplays include *The Night We Never Met* (starring Matthew Broderick and Annabella Sciorra), which he also directed. He was formerly showrunner on *Law & Order: Criminal Intent* and is currently showrunner on HBO's *In Treatment* and a member of the Dramatists Guild Council.

ACKNOWLEDGMENTS

Pay-Per-Kill was first produced by Naked Angels at The Space in New York City as a part of *Naked Rights* (December 6–21, 1991). It was directed by Jace Alexander with the following cast and crew:

GUARD	James Antoine
ELDER BISHOP	Leon Addison Brown
SARAH ANNE	Suzanne Dottino
JOSEPH HOVING	Paul Eckstein
REPORTER	Julianne Hoffenberg
GUARD	Lisa Beth Miller
GOVERNOR	Richard Poe
REPORTER 2	Tim Ransom
DEBORAH ALLEN	Piper Ross
DARYL GATES	Billy Strong
HOST	Bradley White
DENNIS TIM HOKAMP	Garreth Williams
Producer	Jenifer Estess
Coordinating Producer	Julianne Hoffenberg
Scenic Design	George Xenos
Lighting Design	Brian MacDevitt
Costume Design	Rosi Zingales
Sound Design	Guy Sherman, Aural Fixation
Music	Z Power by Recognition Ensemble
Choreography	AZIZA
Lobby Design	Michele Mayas
Stage Manager	Jenny Peek

CAST OF CHARACTERS

HOST
DENNIS TIM HOKAMP
RUDY GIULIANI
HILLARY CLINTON
SHAMUS
FATHER
REPORTER
SARAH ANNE
2ND REPORTER
BISHOP ELDER
GOVERNOR
JOSEPH

PAY-PER-KILL

Music up: big-sporting-event-on-TV fanfare.

Lights up: On a TV press box studio. The kind of box constructed for coverage of a political convention, Monday Night Football, or, as in this case...

HOST. *(Taking cue from an unseen director:)* Hey hey hey, America. It's Friday night. T.G.I.F. Thank God It's...FRY-time. Yes Sirree, the weekend is here and what kind of weekend would it be if you didn't start it out with your weekly, LIVE, PAY! PER! VIEW! EXECUTION! I'm your host, Robin Justice, and along with our whole PAY PER KILL/Court TV team, I'm happy to bring you another FRIDAY NIGHT LIVE AT THE DEATH CHAMBER.

All week long you've heard their stories, you've seen their crimes reenacted, and now you've got just a few minutes left to dial that 900 number at the bottom of the screen to sign on for tonight's show. It's $39.95, and we guarantee a killing. Live. Tonight—

(Lights up on two losers, in separate spaces.)

—one of these two men will die. Crime doesn't pay, and one of these men is going to pay the ultimate price for what he did. And you, the PAY PER KILL audience, will get to be...the hangin' jury. You've got ten seconds left, America, order now. *(Counts it down:)* Six, five, four, three, two, O.K.—half the country has signed up, and the other half is freeloadin'. Next week, watch it on your own sets, folks. Heh heh. O.K.—it's time for the main event. Let's meet our Death Row Boys. First, from Tallahassee, Florida, here for his second week in a row, the little boy who grew up to be quite a menace, Dennis Tom Hokamp, the CIRCLE K KILLER.

(Lights up brighter on DENNIS TOM, an unshaven, 34-year-old white drifter. While the HOST is a TV performer, DENNIS—and all the other guests—are real people who, for a variety of tragic reasons, are now getting their 15 minutes. They do not perform in a fake way.)

HOST. Now Dennis—

DENNIS. *(Interrupting:)* Call me Tom.

HOST. O-kayyy. Tom, as you know, was convicted of robbing several Circle K convenience stores across America, particularly in the southwest. In the course of one or two of those robberies, well, Tom got a little trigger-happy.

(No reply.)

HOST. Didn't you, Tom.

DENNIS. I swear I didn' shoot anyone.

HOST. Still claiming his innocence, all the way to death row.

DENNIS. The people I killed—that was killed, not that I'm admittin' to anything here—but they was mostly Arabs.

HOST. O.K., good point, Tom. Most of them were Arabs. Or at any rate some sort of Third World immigrants. We do have some hidden camera tape *(Looks up at unseen monitor:)* but as Tom's lawyers have pointed out, it's kind of fuzzy, and the action takes place out of camera view *(Winces at something.)* ...for the most part. Now let's give a Pay-Per-Kill welcome to our two experts. First, you can love him, you can hate him, but you have to respect him...MY Mayor and Senatorial candidate, Rudolph Giuliani, and *(Sweet now:)* also this week's guest, you can love her, you can hate her, but you don't have to sleep with her husband, our First Lady, Hillary Rodham Clinton.

> *(Lights up on RUDY and HILLARY. Seated in swivel chairs. Wearing Pay-Per-Kill blazers.)*

HOST. Whichever of these two New Yorkers get to know the least, is the one most likely to get to the Senate.

> *(HILLARY and RUDY force laughs.)*

> *(Note: HILLARY and RUDY are this season's Left/Right, He Says/She Says Couple. If the play is performed next year, please substitute the newest pair of Media Flavors of the Month.)*

RUDY. Good one, Robin. *(Now mimes holding a pistol at audience, or the convicts.)* BANG!... Gotcha.

HOST. Your Honor, Hillary, what do you think of our first mad dog?

RUDY. Ah, ladies first, Ms. Clinton.

HILLARY. This is harder than might first be apparent. I see the defendant, Denni—I mean Thomas's point. The killing itself does take place off screen. And he's with a partner who was never caught. When the government is in a position of taking someone's life. It must be abso—

HOST. Hold on there, Hillary. Mr. Mayor?

RUDY. Thumbs down. He's a lowlife. It doesn't matter who the trigger man was. He was there. Force was used. An eye for an eye. I say fry 'em. It'll be the best thing that ever happened to him. Maybe give him a chance to straighten himself out.

HOST. O.K., folks—a split decision from our judges. Now it's time for you to be the judge. If you want to see Dennis Tom Hokamp go down, call 1-900-CIRCLE K. Your call will be recorded. Now let's move over to the other side of the death row tracks and let's meet 19-year-old Shamus Hoving, from Dewitt, Mississippi. Shamus—

(Lights up on a poor, confused black kid.)

—tried to steal a car in a shopping mall. When the owner showed up, a young pregnant mother of one, a scuffle ensued, and she was shot to death.

SHAMUS. *(Kind of dim:)* She pull the gun. I'm...I'm just really sorry about the whole thing. But I didn't kill her.

HOST. By the way, while trying to make his getaway, Shamus ran over her as well. Judges?

RUDY. This is not the sort of man you just lock up and throw always the key so three years from now he gets probation by some liberal judge and is back on the streets. He shot her in a mall—not in his own neighborhood. Not his own people. What he did to her could happen to any one of our wives. What reason is there for this man to go on living? At taxpayer expense.

HOST. All right, Rudy! Thumbs down twice tonight. Mrs. Clinton?

HILLARY. Well—from what I understand he...he's not necessarily capable of understanding what he did. Um, mentally or emotionally. I know that he comes from a broken home and was—

HOST. Sounds like another split decision, it's gonna be a close one tonight, folks, I can feel it. Dial 1-900-MOM KILL or CIRCLE K. Now, I know a lot of you folks would be happy to see both of these mad dogs die tonight. The only way to put a value on human life is to kill people who don't. But in a civilized society, we all have to make choices, so get to your phones. And cast your votes. By the way, Tom, I understand you plan to get married next week

DENNIS. Yes, I do, sir. The good Lord and the folks out there willing...

HOST. We'll see... Final seconds. Vote. Vote. Vote. You are the jury. And...it's over, folks. And according to our ace statistician, Chip Sorrow—whew, not even close...TOM!—

(This scares the living daylights out of TOM.)

—two weeks in a row, and you're still alive. We'll see you again next week. Maybe the third time will prove the charm.

(Winks at him.)

DENNIS. Sure thing.

HOST. *(Turns now to SHAMUS:)* Barring a last-minute pardon, it looks like it's really over.

(SHAMUS doesn't say anything.)

How do you feel?

SHAMUS. I don' understand.

HOST. Are you sorry now?

(SHAMUS *doesn't respond right away.*)

Would you like to talk to a priest, or a man of the cloth?

SHAMUS. Yes, I think I would.

HOST. Great. While the Reverend makes his way up here, you might take this chance to choose which way you'd like to die.

SHAMUS. (*Not understanding:*) Pardon.

HOST. I don't think so. But you do have a choice between, now listen carefully, lethal injection, firing squad, poison gas, or electric chair.

SHAMUS. (*Nods along slowly:*) Uh, what was the third one?

HOST. Poison gas. Perhaps you'd like to talk it over with your preacher.

SHAMUS. No, I believe I'll go with the gas.

HOST. Gas it is. He's chose the gas, ladies and gentlemen. Now, Shamus, while you sit down for a quick last meal—brought to you by McDonald's, you deserve a break today, so get out and get away to McDonald's—let's have Rudy tell our home viewers about the method of execution you have chosen.

RUDY. Well, as you and our fans know, gas is considered one of the slowest, or slower, ways to go. But perhaps one of the more peaceful. The convict is placed in a sealed room, a sodium cyanide pill is dropped into a canister, where it mixes with acid. Poison gas is produced, and a safe, sensible death ensues.

HOST. No fireworks tonight, then?

RUDY. No—I'm afraid it's a cowardly way out.

HILLARY. Actually, if I recall correctly, gas sometimes doesn't…well, there have been many cases where people have not received enough gas to die easily and they suffer in great pain. Convicted killer Carol Chessman told reporters he would blink if he felt pain (SHAMUS *hears this.*) from the gas, and he blinked throughout his ordeal. Even when it works right it's still inhumane—

HOST. (*Cutting her off:*) O.K., Hillary, thank you. Gas—all in all—a sensible, humane way to go. Shamus, about done with that last meal? (*To audience:*) A McLean burger.

SHAMUS. Well, I…

(*Meal is taken away.* SHAMUS *is lead down Death Row.* HOST *walks alongside.*)

HOST. Folks, it's time for one final walk down that lonesome highway.

(Golf voice:) Shamus. While you're on your way to the gas chamber, we know you'd like to have a few moments with our Father John…just to confess, or to cleanse yourself. A few words between yourself, your minister, your god, and our viewing audience…

FATHER. Bless you, my son.

(They kneel with each other. HOST stays standing.)

HOST. *(Prompts:)* Shamus…

SHAMUS.

I want to tell my mommy I'm sorry for her
She was my mama an I love her
My papa he left me when I was just four
I never seen him
But I know if he's watching
I don't know if he's out there watching
like this
but
maybe. Why did you—
I want my mom.

(HOST signals FATHER to wrap it up. FATHER stands.)

HOST. *(To audience:)* Confession—it's good for the soul. *(To SHAMUS:)* Feel better?

SHAMUS. *(Starts to sing, softly:)*

I'M FRIGHTENED. I'M SORRY.
I'M READY TO DIE.
JESUS HE LOVES ME
MAMA DON'T CRY

I'M SORRY I KILLED HER
I'M SORRY SHE DIED

HOST. *(To audience:)* Just moments to go, folks.

(SHAMUS is led to the chamber as he continues singing.)

SHAMUS.

MY STOMACH IS ACHING, MY MOUTH HAS GONE DRY.
I KNOW THAT I SHOT HER, I JUST DON'T KNOW WHY.

JESUS IS WATCHING
MAMA DON'T CRY
I'M SORRY, I'M SORRY
MAMA DON'T CRY

(He's in the chamber now. Doctor, guards attend to him.)

HOST. *(Repeating—not in song:)* "I'm sorry. I'm sorry. Mama don't cry." With those last words, convicted killer Shamus Hoving is now led into the gas chamber. As he undergoes some last-minute preparations,
> *(Shows him being strapped in place, bolted in.)*

Let's go to the field. First to the home of Circle K killer Dennis Tom Hokamp's fiancée and family, where the feeling is:

REPORTER. One of relief, Robin. You can imagine the tension as the nation voted, and you can imagine the sense of relief when the tally came in. Now, of course, there is also a lingering anxiety.

HOST. Because he still has to come back next week?

REPORTER. That's right. *But,* if he makes it through a third week, his sentence will be commuted to life imprisonment. And with me now, the Circle K killer's fiancée, Sarah Anne. A good night for you?

SARAH ANNE. *(To camera:)* We're very happy. Of course, I'm sad for the Hoving boy, but it's either him or my Tommy, so I just thank the lord he heard our prayers tonight. And thank America for sparing Tommy. He never meant no harm.

REPORTER. And next week? I understand there's a little wedding planned.

SARAH ANNE. *(Beams:)* Yes…on Thursday. At the prison. They won't let him come out.

REPORTER. Do you hope for a long marriage?

SARAH ANNE. Yes, I do. I truly do. He's a good man and I think people, the more they get to know him, they can see that. I have faith… I love you Tommy.

REPORTER. Robin…

HOST. If Tom does survive a third vote, he'll be the first man to escape Death Row since Pay-Per-Kill began. The odds don't look good. Now. How about the family of the Hoving boy? In Dewitt, Mississippi.

2ND REPORTER. Well, there isn't much family left here, and few people remember him. Many people left when the mall opened up and Main Street was shuttered. His father, as he alluded to in has last final confession, left at an early age. His mother is currently in an institution. Still, Council Elder Bishop has agreed to speak for the people of Dewitt:

BISHOP ELDER. Well, we're not proud of what he has done. We jus' want people to know that sort of thing doesn't reflect on the rest of us here. Mostly it's decent law-abiding people. And we all love your show, Robin.

2ND REPORTER. There you have it: the feeling here—embarrassment, concern, and, frankly, a desire to just put this whole tragedy behind them.

HOST. *(Taking his cue:)* Can't blame them, Al. Glad to hear they're fans. To the state capitol with Governor Mervin Thompson. Governor—any chance for a last-minute pardon?

GOVERNOR. I do not think so.

HOST. Really?

GOVERNOR. I'm only sorry we can't fry the both of them tonight. The people of my state want justice. And I want you to know, tomorrow, every school child will see a videotape of tonight's broadcast, because this is how the children will learn.

HOST. Thank you, Governor. By the way—if your kids have wandered from the set, or fallen asleep, now would be a good time to wake them up, because we are one minute away from going live to the gas, and as the governor says—they need to learn right from wrong. As you can see, Shamus is in the chamber now, the doctors have examined him. He's been secured to his chair—we're just moments away. *(To his earpiece:)* What's that? Great. *(To audience:)* We have just found a half-brother of Shamus. We go now to Tacoma, Washington, where Joseph Hoving is standing by. Joseph... What do you think is going through your brother's mind right now?

JOSEPH. *(A little less dim:)* I never, you know, knew him. But I think. I think he look O.K. I think he'll take it like a man.

HOST. Shamus's half-brother, live from Tacoma. And we're live at the Death Chamber, where convicted mom murderer Shamus Hoving waits, strapped in, ready to meet his maker. The clock is ticking down. The Governor's phone is right here in case there's a last-minute change of plans. Five. Four. Three. *(Looks at phone—nothing.)* Two. Killtime!

    (Sound effects of aerosol.)

The pellet has dropped, ladies and gentlemen. Let's just watch...

    (The stage darkens. HOST blacked out. Only SHAMUS, in his chair, in dimmer and dimmer light. His breathing becomes labored. He starts to blink. First a little. Then a lot. Black out.)

End of Play

THROWING YOUR VOICE
by Craig Lucas

BIOGRAPHY

Craig Lucas' plays include *Missing Persons, Blue Window, Reckless, God's Heart, The Dying Gaul, Stranger, Small Tragedy, Prayer For My Enemy,* and *The Singing Forest.* He wrote the book for *The Light In The Piazza,* music and lyrics by Adam Guettel; the musical play *Three Postcards,* music and lyrics by Craig Carnelia; the libretto for the opera *Orpheus in Love,* music by Gerald Busby; and he has recently completed the libretto for *Two Boys,* an opera with composer Nico Muhly, commissioned by the Metropolitan Opera and scheduled to premiere there in a co-production with the English National Opera. His new English adaptations include Brecht's *Galileo,* Chekhov's *Three Sisters* and *Uncle Vanya,* and Strindberg's *Miss Julie.* His screenplays include *Longtime Companion* (Sundance Audience Award), *The Secret Lives of Dentists* (New York Film Critics Best Screenplay), *Prelude to a Kiss, Reckless* and *The Dying Gaul,* which he also directed. Last year Mr. Lucas directed the film *Birds of America.* Onstage he directed Harry Kondoleon's plays *Saved or Destroyed* at Rattlestick (Obie Award for Best Director) and *Play Yourself* as well as his own play *This Thing of Darkness* (co-authored with David Schulner) at the Atlantic. He has worked with directors Bartlett Sher, Norman René, Mark Wing-Davey, Daniel Sullivan, Joe Mantello, Michael Mayer, Lisa Peterson and Anders Cato. His work has been seen on and off Broadway, and at such institutional theaters as Actor's Theatre of Louisville, Berkeley Rep, Cincinnati Playhouse in the Park, Circle Rep, Ensemble Studio Theatre, Goodman, Hartford Stage, Intiman, Lincoln Center, Long Wharf, Manhattan Theatre Club, New York Shakespeare Festival, New York Theatre Workshop, Playwrights Horizons, Portland Stage, Rattlestick, Roundabout, Seattle Rep, South Coast Rep, Steppenwolf, Trinity Rep, and the Vineyard, and it is widely produced internationally. Twice nominated for a Tony (*Prelude to a Kiss* and *The Light in the Piazza*), three times for the Drama Desk (*Prelude, Missing Persons,* and *Reckless*), he has won the L.A. Drama Critics Award (*Blue Window*), the Steinberg/American Theatre Critics Award for Best American Play (*The Singing Forest*), the Hull-Warriner Award (*The Light in the Piazza*), the LAMBDA Literary Award (for his anthology *What I Meant Was*), the Flora Roberts Award, the Excellence in Literature Award from the American Academy of Arts and Letters, the Laura Pels/PEN Mid-Career Achievement Award and the Joan Cullman Award; he has twice won the Obie Award for Best Play (*Prelude* and *Small Tragedy*). He graduated from Boston University where he studied with poets Anne Sexton and George Starbuck. Mr. Lucas serves as Associate Artistic Director at the Intiman Theatre in Seattle, and he is a member of the Dramatists Guild, the Writers Guild of America, the Directors Guild, SSDC and PEN America. He lives in upstate New York.

ACKNOWLEDGMENTS

Throwing Your Voice was first produced by Naked Angels at The Space in New York City as a part of *Naked Rights* (December 6–21, 1991). It was directed by Jace Alexander and Paul S. Eckstein with the following cast:

RICHARD	Tim Ransom
LUCY	Jennifer Estess
DOUG	David Marshall Grant
SARAH	Lisa Beth Miller

And the following production staff:

Producer	Jenifer Estess
Coordinating Producer	Julianne Hoffenberg
Scenic Design	George Xenos
Lighting Design	Brian MacDevitt
Costume Design	Rosi Zingales
Sound Design	Guy Sherman, Aural Fixation

CAST OF CHARACTERS

RICHARD

LUCY

DOUG

SARAH

LITTLE SOUTH AFRICAN GIRL'S VOICE

TIME AND PLACE

After dinner. 1991.

To Michael Bronski.

THROWING YOUR VOICE

After dinner. LUCY, DOUG, and RICHARD have coffee; SARAH has herbal tea. She is hugely pregnant. Gentle music plays on the sound system; it will end at some point and no one will rise to put on another CD.

RICHARD. Yeah, but to have them killed? Or maimed?

LUCY. *(To SARAH, offering honey:)* Honey?

(SARAH shakes her head.)

RICHARD. To *pay* somebody to do that for you? I mean, I understand killing somebody in the heat of passion. Or if they had something you had to have.

LUCY. They did.

DOUG. But they did.

RICHARD. Yeah, I guess… But, no, I guess I actually have no trouble imagining killing somebody when they walk in the middle of the subway stairs in front of you really slowly—

LUCY. Yes.

RICHARD. —and are just incredibly fat— *(To SARAH:)* Not you. These people have eaten themselves to this— *(To them:)* And, you know, you try to go this way, they move—

DOUG. Right.

LUCY. They're doing it on purpose, just to incense you.

(Pause. The music plays.)

DOUG. …Or those jerks who block the aisles at Food Emporium, staring at some foodstuff—

RICHARD. Those are the ones.

DOUG. —as if they'd just woken up from a fifty-year sleep and are trying to pick the really—right…

LUCY. They're having a stroke, probably.

DOUG. *(Overlapping slightly:)* …brie… No, they're not having a stroke. Why would you take their side? I hate those people.

(LUCY smiles.)

LUCY. You're right. They should die.

RICHARD. I just…I don't know…to *pay* somebody…to kill the mother of your daughter's main competition for the cheerleaders so she'll be too distraught to audition… It worries me.

DOUG. Well, it's passive-aggressive.

LUCY. It is.

RICHARD. *(To* SARAH:*)* Are we going to be like that in sixteen years?

SARAH. Mm-hm.

RICHARD. Plotting...living our entire lives through little Grendel? Having no life of our own?

LUCY. She should've killed the daughter's friend directly.

DOUG. That would've—

LUCY. That would've been healthier.

DOUG. Don't you think? Little Grendel? Is that what you call it?

RICHARD. Mm-hm.

LUCY. But...you know...if I think about it...I would probably...if I thought I could get away with it?

DOUG. Uh-huh?

LUCY. I would do the exact same thing to Orrin Hatch and Arlen Specter.

SARAH. Yes.

LUCY. Wouldn't you?

(SARAH nods.)

Kill their mothers so they're too distraught to go the Senate.

SARAH. Yes. Or...actually I've thought about it...and I would make them... take old rusty fishing knives used for cleaning, you know...squid—

LUCY. Mm-hm.

SARAH. —or... And I would make them cut each other's tongues out and eat them live on television while Anita Hill stands over them and...

LUCY. Screams.

SARAH. No... Actually, I would have her, I mean, I think it would be the best if she just, you know, *shit* in their bloody mouths. Don't you?

(Tiny beat before:)

RICHARD. Dinner was delicious, thanks... Being pregnant has brought out such a warmth of fellow feeling in Sarah.

LUCY. No, come on. They're horrible people.

RICHARD. It's very moving. Yes, they are. Horrible. *(Beat; to* DOUG *and* SARAH:*)* What is this?

LUCY. It's... *(She looks at* DOUG.*)*

SARAH. It's beautiful

DOUG. Schubert?

LUCY. Schumann?

RICHARD. One of the Shoe People. No, don't get up.

(*LUCY moves toward the sound system.*)

LUCY. No, I wanted to get some water. Anybody else?

RICHARD. No, thank you.

SARAH. No. Thanks.

LUCY (*Overlapping:*) Schumann.

RICHARD. Schumann?

DOUG. But…

LUCY. Doug?

DOUG. No. Thanks. But…if you think about it?

RICHARD. Mm-hm?

DOUG. Like the woman in Texas? She wanted what she wanted but she didn't want to—

SARAH. Right.

RICHARD. Exactly.

DOUG. It's like…I don't particularly…

LUCY. (*Returning with water:*) What is this?

DOUG. I was saying…

SARAH. The woman in Texas.

DOUG. I don't particularly want, say, to go to Iraq and kill a hundred thousand Iraqis even if I do think their president is…

RICHARD. A menace.

DOUG. Well, I don't know what I think, because Iraq is one of the few countries in the Middle East that isn't in the Middle Ages. I mean, women don't have to walk around with bags on their faces and people can vote, can't they?

RICHARD. I don't know.

DOUG. But…anyway, I don't want to see the faces of the people, the children, we kill.

RICHARD. Right.

DOUG. So I pay taxes to a government which pays an entire underclass to go—

RICHARD. (*Simultaneously:*) Right.

SARAH. (*Simultaneously:*) Right.

DOUG. —and do it for me, so I can still have my air conditioning in the summer.

LUCY. Which, of course, we don't have.

DOUG. I mean, it's sort of the same. It's still murder.

LUCY. I think that's ridiculous.

DOUG. I know you do.

LUCY. *(Overlapping:)* I'm sorry. I think if we hadn't done it he would have eventually blown us all to smithereens or we would have all—history would have been set back centuries by this crazy man and the Iraqi people—*Wait*—are responsible for their actions and their own nation and I'm sorry they're all dead. That's all.

    (Pause.)

DOUG. My point…was only that…we often…people often pay other people to do their dirty work so they don't have to look at the consequences—

LUCY. Yes.

DOUG. —of their actions.

LUCY. I don't think it was dirty work. I think…

DOUG. It was God's work?

LUCY. We don't agree on this subject.

    (Pause.)

RICHARD. But…you know? Okay: one way, too, of looking at it is that people…if everyone was actually responsible for their own actions and—

DOUG. Well—

RICHARD. —nothing else. If the woman in Texas were not held responsible, even though she paid this guy—

DOUG. Legally?

RICHARD. Legally, morally, any way. If… See, I didn't go to Iraq.

DOUG. But you paid taxes.

RICHARD. Yes. But—

DOUG. And you *pay* taxes—

LUCY. Let him finish.

DOUG. Wait, you pay taxes to support a government that practices murder in this state. Capital punishment.

LUCY. *(Simultaneously:)* There's no capital—

RICHARD. *(Simultaneously:)* Not in New York.

DOUG. No?

LUCY. There's no death penalty in New York State.

RICHARD. No.

DOUG. *(Overlapping:)* Are you sure? That's right.

LUCY. *(Overlapping:)* Not for twenty years.

DOUG. Well, there goes my argument. But...I mean— *(To SARAH:)* Would you buy fur?

SARAH. With what?

DOUG. If you could?...

SARAH. If I could? No.

DOUG. No? Would you buy...?

LUCY. I would. And I would wear it in grandeur.

DOUG. We know you would. But you're poor and you'll always be poor... W—?

LUCY. *(Singing:)* Marat we're poor,
And the poor stay poor.

DOUG. That's right.

SARAH *(Overlapping:)* Right!

(SARAH joins her and they sing together:)

LUCY and SARAH. Marat don't make us wait anymore!
We want our rights!

DOUG. Thank you!

LUCY. *(Singing:)* And we don't—

(SARAH has momentarily forgotten the words; she rejoins LUCY on:)

LUCY and SARAH. *(Singing:)* —care how!
We want our revolution!
Now!

(LUCY and SARAH crack up.)

DOUG. Yes, me too. All right...

LUCY. I can't believe it!

DOUG. Just tell me: would you buy—

LUCY. *(Mouthed, silently:)* I still know those words.

SARAH. I know!

DOUG. *(Overlapping:)* Would you buy coffee from Columbia if you knew— *(To LUCY:)* Where is this coffee from?

LUCY. D'Agostino.

DOUG. If you knew people had died...culling it.

LUCY. Harvesting.

SARAH. No, I suppose...

RICHARD. But wait.

LUCY. Culling?

RICHARD. *(Overlapping:)* Wait, wait.

LUCY. Dougie, you always do this. It was so peaceful here.

DOUG. We're not having a bad time. Are we?

SARAH. No.

RICHARD. No.

LUCY. But you're gonna make all the people feel bad. They're gonna go home—

DOUG. No, they're not.

LUCY. —feeling guilty and defiled and sorry they weren't born in Ghana.

RICHARD. But. I just… Here's my point.

LUCY. Okay.

DOUG. Okay.

RICHARD. If people were responsible for their own actions alone…

DOUG. NO one's unhappy.

RICHARD. If the soldiers who went to Iraq—

DOUG. I understand.

RICHARD. —were wholly responsible for their going there and I didn't feel any responsibility whatsoever.

DOUG. But you're saying that you do.

RICHARD. Yes, I do. But I'm als— I'm saying that's stupid. Even if I agreed that it was entirely wrong for them to go there which…I don't know about—

DOUG. You don't.

RICHARD. No. But let's say…I voted for George Bush and I supported the war…totally…

DOUG. Okay.

RICHARD. I still…in an existential way…don't think I should be responsible for someone else's actions.

> *(Pause.)*

DOUG. Would you invest in South Africa?

RICHARD. No. Well, yes, I shouldn't—I already have.

> *(Beat.)*

DOUG. Have—?

RICHARD. That's probably where…I mean, I don't know, that's probably where Sarah's ring is from. I didn't ask when I bought it, I was all of twenty-two. *(Pause.)* But… *(He looks at SARAH.)* I've read that most diamonds, new diamonds come from there.

(Pause.)

DOUG. Well, okay.

LUCY. It is okay, don't say it like that.

RICHARD. I also read that...people are killed in the diamond mines. Children, for all I know. It's horrible. And I didn't know. What are we supposed to do? *(He looks at* SARAH.*)* I'm sorry. It's probably not. I'm just... for the sake of argument—

DOUG. *(Overlapping slightly:)* Okay. But would you buy ivory then?

RICHARD. No. But I also wouldn't throw away *old ivory,* if I had it.

DOUG. You wouldn't?

RICHARD. No.

DOUG. Why?

RICHARD. Because I think the damage is already done.

DOUG. But then you're saying there is damage.

RICHARD. No—

DOUG. I caught you! You admit—

RICHARD. No, I'm saying, *if* there's damage, if you're right, which I don't agree with—

DOUG. You do and you don't, you mean.

LUCY. Arlen Specter here.

RICHARD. The damage, you've already paid for the ivory or the diamond or—

DOUG. But if you keep it and treat it as if it's precious, somebody else could sell it someday, thus contributing to the ivory market, thus contributing rather directly to the slaughter of elephants.

RICHARD. Well, I think that's kind of...a long chain of command.

DOUG. But it is that. You're still in command. You sell that diamond someday, if it's from South Africa—

RICHARD. Oh, come on, look—

LUCY. Doug.

(Pause.)

DOUG. What?

(Pause.)

RICHARD. I think...when you boycott a nation, the entire economy suffers. Including the poor people.

(Silence, the music has ended.)

And I don't think…because I buy a diamond…I mean, first of all it's the only thing I've ever bought that's worth anything.

DOUG. Fine.

SARAH. Don't get defensive.

RICHARD. I'm not. Have you ever taken it off, though? In eight years?

(She shakes her head.)

LUCY. Ohhh. That's so romantic.

SARAH. I don't think I could get if off now.

(She tries to test it; RICHARD stops her.)

RICHARD. Don't. You'll break the spell. *(Pause.)* Though you'll probably have to when the baby comes, because we're gonna probably need the money.

LUCY. Ohhhh.

RICHARD. I mean… Is that what we should do?

DOUG. No, Richard.

RICHARD. If… Here. If I knew for certain…for *sure* that someone had actually died in the mining of this diamond. A little thirteen year old black girl…a *pregnant* thirteen year old black girl—

LUCY. Oh, please.

RICHARD. —who had to work in the kitchen of one of the mines… and she stole a sliver of diamond, this very diamond, to pay for the baby… and was beaten for it…beaten to death. *(Pause.)* Should I get rid of the diamond? *Not* sell it because that would contribute to the diamond mine?

DOUG. I—

RICHARD. Should we just…throw it in the gutter?

(Pause.)

DOUG. I wouldn't presume to tell—

RICHARD. Where are your *shoes* from, Doug? Where was this wonderful meal grown? Do you know? Do you check all the labels?

DOUG. No.

(Pause. No one moves.)

LUCY. Look, let's everybody kiss and—

(SARAH's head makes a sudden, sharp turn.)

What? Are you okay?

(SARAH nods.)

RICHARD. That's all. I'm just…

DOUG. I understand.

LUCY. So—

RICHARD. I mean— …I'm sorry. I guess you hit a nerve. *(To* LUCY:*)* What? Kiss and make up. Yes.

(He makes a kissing noise at DOUG.*)*

DOUG. *(Overlapping:)* We're not fighting. You can't stand it if people disagree. Unless it's you.

*(*DOUG *makes a kissing noise at* RICHARD.*)*

RICHARD. My father left me exactly twenty-five thousand dollars in his will and I went out and bought the diamond for Sarah. That was all the money I've ever had at one time and probably ever will.

(Pause.)

SARAH. Does anyone hear that? …I'm sorry.

RICHARD. What?

SARAH. Like…a *voice?*

RICHARD. Time to go.

SARAH. Stop! Don't everyone look at me like I'm Joan of Arc. Ever since I gave up caffeine and alcohol, I have this buzzing. *That.*

(They all listen.)

DOUG. I know what it is. *(He stands.)* I hear it too.

SARAH. You do?

DOUG. Yes. It's the stereo.

LUCY. That's right.

DOUG. It picks up the police signals.

SARAH. Oh, thank god. Uh! *(She sighs with great relief.)*

RICHARD. What did you think the voice was saying?

SARAH. It was screaming, actually.

RICHARD. It was?

SARAH. Yes.

RICHARD. My little mystic. *(He takes her hand in his.)*

SARAH. God.

RICHARD. That was probably Joan of Arc's problem, she was picking up the police signals. Don't you think?

LUCY. It drives me crazy. We hear it all hours. It doesn't even have to be on.

DOUG. Yes, it does. *(He sits back down.)*

RICHARD. Okay?

*(*SARAH *smiles, weakly. Then, her expression changes.)*

What...? You still...?

> (SARAH *looks down at her hand in* RICHARD's *hand; she pulls her hand free and sees the ring. She lifts it to her ear. She gasps.*)

Oh very funny. Fine, get rid of the ring, I don't care.

SARAH. *(Overlapping:)* "Don't hit me!" Listen! *(She holds the ring out to* RICHARD.*)* Listen to it!

RICHARD. Yeah, I'm sure.

SARAH. I'm sorry, I hear something, I can't help it.

> (LUCY *takes* SARAH's *hand and leans in, listening to the ring. At the same time:*)

RICHARD. No, it's fine.

> (SARAH *listens again, then covers the ring with her other hand.*)

You all have your little joke.

> (LUCY *shakes her head; she doesn't hear it.*)

It's been a lovely evening. Thanks.

SARAH. You don't...?

> (SARAH *puts the ring to her ear again. Softly at first, we hear:*)

LITTLE SOUTH AFRICAN GIRL'S VOICE. Don't hit me! Please don't hit me!

SARAH. Nobody hears that?

RICHARD. I think we should go.

> *(The tiny voice screams a bloodcurdling scream.)*

LITTLE SOUTH AFRICAN GIRL'S VOICE. Please! Please god! Don't hit me!

> (SARAH *tears at her finger, removing the ring and throwing it down. The voice screams without words under:*)

RICHARD. What are you...?

SARAH. I don't want it! I don't want the ring! Get rid of it.

LITTLE SOUTH AFRICAN GIRL'S VOICE. Please!

SARAH. You can *keep* it!

RICHARD. Okay.

LITTLE SOUTH AFRICAN GIRL'S VOICE. Please don't hit me! Help! Help me, god! Please god.

> *(The others stare at* SARAH, *who looks back at them. The tiny voice continues screaming as the lights fade.)*

End of Play

naked
angels
takes on
women

FRUITS AND NUTS
A COMIC DUET

by Ned Eisenberg

BIOGRAPHY

Ned Eisenberg is an actor-playwright who lives in NYC. His work has been performed in New York, Philadelphia, and Los Angeles and he's had two plays at the O'Neill Playwrights Conference. He is a member of Ensemble Studio Theatre and the Actor's Workshop Company as well as one of the founding members of Naked Angels and a Fox Fellowship recipient.

ACKNOWLEDGMENTS

Fruits and Nuts was first produced by Naked Angels at The Space in New York City as a part of *Naked Angels Takes on Women* (March 10–April 10, 1993). It was directed by Joumana Rizk with the following cast:

WOMAN .... Laura Salvato
MAN .... Ned Eisenberg

And the following production staff:

Artistic Directors .... Liz Diamond, Toni Kotite
Producers .... Jenifer Estess, Rachael Horovitz
Coordinating Producer .... Julianne Hoffenberg
Scenic Design .... William F. Moser
Lighting Design .... Jeanne Koenig, John Paul Szczepaski
Costume Design .... Cynthia A. Clemmons
Sound Design .... Roger Raines
Casting .... Brett Goldstein
Special Performance Director .... Melinda Wade
Literature Coordinator .... Valerie Estess
Company Artistic Representatives .... Frank Pugliese,
Fisher Stevens

CAST OF CHARACTERS

WOMAN, late twenties or early thirties

MAN, late twenties or early thirties

SETTING

A room in a city apartment.

TIME

Now. And forever.

NOTE

This play is written in free verse and prose with minimal punctuation. Feel free to "sing" the play and "dance" it as well. The emotions of the characters are enormous, operatic, raw, and comically indulgent in their passionate intensity and therefore the physical and vocal styling of the players must rise to the occasion.

FRUITS AND NUTS

The lights rise on a MAN *and a* WOMAN. *The* MAN *sits immobile in a chair. The* WOMAN *is on her feet. The only props and set pieces of any import are a large bowl of fresh cut fruit and a telephone. The fruit salad consists of kiwi, strawberries, pineapple spears, and other fruit filler.*

WOMAN. This is over, do you hear me, do you hear me?!!
This is it, this is it! I need a man, a man!!
Not a boy, not a teenager, not some "guy!"
You are a guy, not a man, and I need a man to share my life with!
I curse the day I met you
You stubborn selfish piece of shit
I hate you so much it kills me
I foam at the mouth like a rabid beast from you
Are you happy, you're free
And you'll die free
Alone and poor and sick with no one to take care of you
I hate you!
But I hate me more for being with you
Everyone thinks I'm nuts
Your neighbors don't like you
The girl with the shepherd mutt down the street
Thinks you're a creep and she doesn't even know you
Everyone says YOU SUCK!
You're not good looking, you're not rich,
There's nothing special about you at all!
Why do I let you do this?!
Just look at what you do to me!!
Oh God, why have I been punished so long?!

(Short pause.)

I don't want to see you anymore
I want you out of my life
I don't want to hear what you have to say
Not that you ever have something to say
Just the same old uncommitted empty words
"Maybe, who knows, we'll see!"
I'm sorry I let you inside me
My mouth, my hands, my guts are filthy from you
I *sceeve* you, you ugly hateful bastard
You and your whole family

And your people and your gang
And everything connected to you!
You have no trust in you
You have no love in you
You finally got what you want
You won
Be happy
Call all your deadbeat friends who hate me
Have a party, fuck some bimbos!
I want my pictures back!

> *(She dashes offstage into another room. We hear her banging about. The MAN impulsively bolts up from the chair, clenching his fists, ready to attack. She re-enters empty handed. They look at one another. He sits back down. She resumes.)*

I don't want your tacky bitches with my pictures
You'd probably throw them out though, wouldn't you
Destroy the evidence, wouldn't you
You know what, I really don't care
They're nothing
You're nothing
This whole thing is nothing
I hope you have a good life
I hope you get what you think you need
Any shit of mine that's here
Tear it up, burn it down, throw it out
It's poisoned
Diseased
Condemned
Like everything else in this sick dead relationship!

> *(She exits the apartment. He sits there in silence surveying the room and digesting all he's just heard. After a short while, the phone starts to ring. With each ring we see the MAN's anger start to bubble up inside him till the fifth ring when he unleashes it in his "aria." The phone rings intermittently throughout his tirade.)*

MAN. You fucking bitch, what do you want?!
More than four rings, that's gotta be you
You're sorry? Again?
Apologize? Again?!
Stick ice picks in my ears, then take 'em out?!
If you get mad, stay mad, or don't get mad at all,

You dopey, foul mouth, venomous cunt!
Is this your P.M.S., your M.S., or your post motherfucking M.S. that's to
    blame this time!
Come back, come back,
Come back I'll see you bleed from your face
As well as your snatch, you miserable lousy shit!

Rule of thumb, English law, rule of thumb!
A man can beat his wife
With a club as thick as his thumb
Break my heart and twist my intestines, for what
For what you kill me with aggravation
What did I ever do to you?!!
        (The phone stops ringing. He stops speaking. It starts ringing again.)
Nut job, screwball, useless, good-for-nothing piece of shit!
I have no trust and I'm uncommitted, huh?
I wonder why!
I'd have to be certified mad
To saddle myself to a psycho like you!
In Rio, they'd chop you up for this abuse
In India, douse you with oil and roast you alive!
Now I know why Arabs veil your mouths
To make sure you shut the fuck up!!
        (The phone stops ringing.)
I don't want to see you
Or hear you
Or smell you or taste you or touch you again
Don't be sorry, don't be sweet, don't call and act coy
Don't write me on lovely blank cards
I'd cut off my dick before I'd fuck you now!
You!
No more will you have it so good
Ungrateful bitch that you are
So wander the earth, hungry and wet,
And get out of my life and die!
        (—the phone starts ringing yet again in the middle of the last line—)
And stop with the phone, you crazy cunt, you wacko bitch!
        *(The phone stops ringing as the MAN throws himself into a heap on the
        floor. After a few moments, the buzzer from the downstairs door starts to
        ring. The MAN gets up from the floor and collects himself but doesn't go to
        ring back. The ringing continues intermittent, yet unabated. The MAN then*

starts to physically battle himself to keep from ringing back and letting her in. After a Herculean struggle between his body and his better judgment, his body wins and he is physically compelled to open the door for her as he has a thousand times before. The WOMAN *walks in with one shoe on and the other shoe and its heel in her hand. Pause.)*

WOMAN. Why didn't you answer the phone? *(Pause.)* My heel broke. Again. Cheap shit fucking shoe.

(She brings the shoe and heel to him and holds it out for him to take. He doesn't.)

Come on, help me. Get over it, will you? Be a man.

(He doesn't take it.)

Fix it and I'll leave. Please. Please.

(He snatches it from her and starts to repair the shoe with the Krazy Glue he keeps in his pocket.)

Don't be mad. You know I love you. You make me angry sometimes. I'm sorry.

(He works on the shoe in silence.)

Don't ignore me. Please say something. Please.

MAN. …There's nothing to say.

WOMAN. …You said something.

(She starts eating the fruit salad from the bowl while she watches him fix her footwear. She smiles lovingly at him and coyly laughs. He's not amused or is at least giving the impression of not being amused. She takes a cut strawberry and puts the two halves together to form what looks like a vagina. She shows it to him.)

Look.

(She gets up and brings the berries to his face.)

Lick it. Eat it.

(He swings his head away from the fruit and growls his response—)

MAN. Go on.

WOMAN. *(Imitating:)* Go on.

(She takes one of the strawberry halves and eats it. The other half she fits onto the bridge of her nose. She balances it and starts to sing in either Asian or Arabic sounding gibberish while doing an odalisque's dance around the room. The MAN *reluctantly smiles to himself and although she doesn't see this she senses it just the same. She takes the fruit off her nose and comes to him.)*

Gimme your face.

MAN. Whadaya want?

WOMAN. Your face. Gimme your face.

> *(He allows her to gently tilt his head back. She places the strawberry half on his nose.)*

MAN. Whadaya doin'?

WOMAN. Fruitface, sssh.

> *(She takes kiwi slices from the fruit bowl.)*

Close your eyes.

> *(He does and she tenderly places one kiwi slice over each of his eyelids.)*

Open your mouth for me.

MAN. Why?

WOMAN. Please. Open your mouth for me.

> *(He does and she takes a pineapple spear, sucks off the excess juice, and puts it in his mouth pointing straight out from between his teeth. She then eats the kiwi slices off his eyes and the berry from his nose. He's left with the pineapple in his mouth. He looks at her. She then eats the pineapple up to his lips. He eats the rest. They look at each other. A silence, a beat, and then impulsively, at the same second, they clutch and kiss. Tableau.)*

End of Play

WHAT WE'RE UP AGAINST
by Theresa Rebeck

BIOGRAPHY

Theresa Rebeck is a widely produced playwright throughout the United States and abroad. Past New York productions of her work include *Mauritius* at the Biltmore Theatre in a Manhattan Theater Club Production; *The Scene, The Water's Edge, Loose Knit, The Family of Mann* and *Spike Heels* at Second Stage; *Bad Dates, The Butterfly Collection* and *Our House* at Playwrights Horizons; and *View of the Dome* at New York Theatre Workshop. *Omnium Gatherum* (co-written, finalist for the Pulitzer Prize in 2003) was featured at the Humana Festival, and had a commercial run at the Variety Arts Theatre. Her newest work, *The Understudy*, will open in New York at the Laura Pels Theater at the Roundabout in the Fall of 2009.

All of Ms. Rebeck's past produced plays are published by Smith and Kraus as *Theresa Rebeck: Complete Plays, Volumes I, II* and *III* and in acting editions available from Samuel French. Ms. Rebeck's other publications are *Free Fire Zone*, a book of comedic essays about writing and show business. She has written for *American Theatre Magazine* and has had excerpts of her plays published in the *Harvard Review*. Ms. Rebeck's first novel, *Three Girls and Their Brother*, was published by Random House/Shaye Areheart Books and is available online and at fine booksellers everywhere.

In television, Ms. Rebeck has written for *Dream On, Brooklyn Bridge, L.A. Law, American Dreamer, Maximum Bob, First Wave*, and *Third Watch*. She has been a writer/producer for *Canterbury's Law, Smith, Law and Order: Criminal Intent* and *NYPD Blue*. Her produced feature films include *Harriet the Spy, Gossip*, and the independent feature *Sunday on the Rocks*. Awards include the Mystery Writer's of America's Edgar Award, the Writer's Guild of America award for Episodic Drama, the Hispanic Images Imagen Award, and the Peabody, all for her work on NYPD Blue. She has won the National Theatre Conference Award (for *The Family of Mann*), and was awarded the William Inge New Voices Playwriting Award in 2003 for *The Bells. Mauritius* was originally produced at Boston's Huntington Theatre, where it received the 2007 IRNE Award for Best New Play as well as the Eliot Norton Award.

Ms. Rebeck is originally from Cincinnati and holds an MFA in Playwriting and a PhD. in Victorian Melodrama, both from Brandeis University. She is a proud board member of the Dramatists Guild and has taught at Brandeis University and Columbia University. She lives in Brooklyn with her husband Jess Lynn and two children, Cooper and Cleo.

ACKNOWLEDGMENTS

What We're Up Against was first produced by Naked Angels at The Space in New York City as a part of *Naked Angels Takes on Women* (March 10–April 10, 1993). It was directed by Susann Brinkley with the following cast:

STU .... Fisher Stevens

BEN .... Billy Strong

And the following production staff:

Artistic Directors .... Liz Diamond, Toni Kotite

Producers .... Jenifer Estess, Rachael Horovitz

Coordinating Producer .... Julianne Hoffenberg

Scenic Design .... William F. Moser

Lighting Design .... Jeanne Koenig, John Paul Szczepaski

Costume Design .... Cynthia A. Clemmons

Sound Design .... Roger Raines

Casting .... Brett Goldstein

Special Performance Director .... Melinda Wade

Literature Coordinator .... Valerie Estess

Company Artistic Representatives .... Frank Pugliese,
Fisher Stevens

CAST OF CHARACTERS

STU, White, thirty

BEN, White, thirty

SETTING

An office.

WHAT WE'RE UP AGAINST

STU and BEN *sit at a drafting table.* STU *reaches into the bottom drawer of a file cabinet, finds a bottle of scotch, and pours drinks.*

STU. All I'm saying is there's—

BEN. Rules. That's what I'm trying to—

STU. A system.

BEN. Yes, Jesus, I—

STU. Things don't just happen, history, events—

BEN. I know, this is not—

STU. We create.

BEN. Exactly. A company. I tried to—

STU. You look at anything, the boy scouts, some fucking convent, and maybe it doesn't seem like—

BEN. You just can't—

STU. It's part of something much more complicated. You can't just act like that's not true.

BEN. That's my point. She's a fucking bitch. That's all I'm saying.

STU. I'm not saying that. That is not what—

BEN. Okay, okay, fine, but—

STU. You cannot give them that.

BEN. I'm not giving them anything. I'm just saying, she doesn't belong. I don't know why they hired another fucking woman, it's not like—

STU. Look, they want to work, women want to work, they should have the opportunity. I'm not saying—fuck, that's just—you know that's what they think, they all have their little meetings and tell each other that we don't want them, we're threatened, when that's not the issue. You can't give them that. Because that's not the problem.

BEN. Stu, you just said she—

STU. She tricked me. The bitch tricked me, that is my point. She is a lying, deceitful, dishonest little manipulator. I don't mind working with her. But, she is a cunt. That, I mind.

BEN. That's what I'm—

STU. No, that is not what you're saying, Ben. These are two very different things. I welcomed her. I was happy when they hired her, I said, I want to work with this woman.

BEN. Oh, come on—

STU. Excuse me?

BEN. What? I'm just saying—

STU. What are you saying, Ben?

BEN. I'm saying, shit, I'm saying you didn't want her any more than the rest of us. What do we need another woman for? Janice is, we have one of them, I don't know what—

STU. This isn't an issue of sex. That's what I'm telling you. Are you fucking listening to me?

BEN. Yes, I'm listening, you're not—

STU. It's the system I'm talking about. It's not whether or not she's a woman. It's the fact that she has no respect, this is my point. She comes into my office and says, we need to talk, Stu, and I'm, okay, I'm fine, I can talk, I don't have a problem with this. She has questions. I'm fine with this. She wants to know why I won't let her work. Now, that is not what is happening, I explain that to her. She is a new employee, how long has she been here, five months, six months, this is not—the experience isn't there. That is my point. When the experience is there, she'll be put on projects. She wants to know how she can get the experience if we won't let her work. This is a good question. And so I tell her: Initiative. Initiative, that is how the system works, that is how America works, this is what they don't understand. No one hands you things. You work for them. You earn them. You prove yourself worthy. So she says to me, what about Webber? And I say, what about him? And she says, you let him work. He's been here four months, and you put him on projects.

BEN. Oh, that fucking—

STU. Exactly. She's jealous. The bitch is jealous. She doesn't care about the work, she just cares, she's competitive, Webber got ahead of her and she doesn't like it. She's after his balls. So I say to her, that's got nothing to do with you. Nothing. This isn't about competition. This is about business. We use the best person for the job. If you prove yourself, through initiative, to be the best person, to be worthy, we will use you.

BEN. So what'd she say to—

STU. I'll tell you what she said. This fucking bitch, she stopped by Webber's office and picked up a copy of that mall extension you guys are working on, the Roxbury project—

BEN. What? What'd she do that for?

STU. So she's got your design, right—

BEN. That thing's not finished, Stu. Did she show you that? She had no business doing that. We are not finished with that.

STU. So she says to me—

BEN. I cannot believe that bitch, trying to make us look bad! We haven't solved the duct thing yet, okay, we're still working on it! I can't believe—

STU. Would you shut up, Ben? I'm trying to explain something to you. She's not after your balls, she's after Webber—

BEN. I'm just saying, we're still working on that. We've got ideas.

STU. I'm not talking about your ideas, Ben, I'm trying to tell you something! She brings me your design, she tells me she got it from Webber, and then she says, I can see putting Ben on this, he's got seniority. But why does Webber get to work, and not me? What is so good about what he does? Tell me why Webber got this project and not me. She's pissing me off now, because I explained this to her, it's not about competition, I said that, but if she wants to play this game, fine, fuck her, I'll show her why Webber got the project. So I go through it. Every detail. I show her how every fucking detail indicates that Webber has experience. I prove it to her. And you know what she says to me? "I designed that."

BEN. What?

STU. The bitch put Webber's name on one of her designs. She came up with her own fucking design for that fucking mall, and then she pretended it was Webber's. She tricked me.

BEN. You're shitting me.

STU. This fucking woman stands there—she stands there, and says to me, "This is my point, Stu. It's not about the work, it's about point of view. When a woman designs it, it's shit, and when a man designs it, it's great." So I say to her, no this isn't about point of view, this is about power, you fucking bitch. You're trying to cut off my balls here. She says, look at the design, Stu, you know it's good, and I say, I don't give a shit if it's good. You want to play by these rules, I can play by these rules. It's shit. Get out of my face.

BEN. You said that?

STU. She says, I want to work. Why won't you let me work? And I say fuck you. What you want is power. You fucking cunt, don't lie to me. You come in here and try and cut off my balls, I welcomed you, and this is what you do.

BEN. Fucking bitch.

STU. This is what we're up against.

BEN. Fuck.

(*Pause. They think about this.*)

BEN. But it was good?

STU. What?

BEN. The design. You said—

STU. Fuck you, are you fucking listening to a word I'm saying?

BEN. Yes, I'm listening, I just—I was wondering what she did with the air ducts.

STU. What? What are you saying?

BEN. I'm saying, you know, Webber and I—those fucking ducts are all over the entryway there, and we can't—

STU. Fuck you, Ben, you are not listening to a word out of my mouth.

BEN. Yeah, I know, she's a cunt, I'm just saying, you said the design was good, so I was just wondering—

STU. The design is shit.

BEN. Yeah, but if she's got an idea—

STU. She's got nothing, Ben. Nothing. You give her nothing.

BEN. Why not?

STU. Excuse me? What? Excuse me?

BEN. If she's got one fucking idea—

STU. She tricked me.

BEN. Yeah, but you don't let her work, Stu. She's right about that. You let Janice do more, and her work is for shit.

STU. What are you—what is your fucking point, Ben?

BEN. I don't have a point! I just want to see that fucking design. Webber and I have been going over that fucking duct thing for weeks and we can't crack it. So, if she's got a solution, I want to see it. Did she have a solution or not?

STU. Yeah. She did.

BEN. Well, I want to see it.

STU. No.

BEN. She's here now, fuck, they hired her and we had nothing to say about it, she's being paid, why shouldn't we use her?

STU. I'll tell you why. Because then, she's won. She didn't wait. She didn't play by the rules. It's context. If she had waited, it would've been different. If she had respect for the system. But she has no respect. This is what we're up against.

BEN. That's a load of shit, Stu.

STU. I'm what? Excuse me, did you, what did you—

BEN. Look, Stu—

STU. If she were here, listening to us, you know what she'd do?

BEN. Hopefully, she'd tell me what she did with those fucking ducts—

STU. No. That is not what she'd do. I'll tell you what she'd do. Two men, having a simple conversation, we're having drinks. Right? Is there anything wrong with this? But she sits here and she listens to us, and then she goes and tells her little friends. She goes back to her little group, and she says, "They said this, and they said that, they called me a bitch, they called me a cunt" and she and her friends, they all act like this is some big fucking point. But there is no point, Ben. This is what they don't understand. There is a system. Things fit together. It's not about point of view. It's just about the way things are. They want things to be the way they're not. They don't get it, and they're trying to make us pay for that. But they are not going to win. It's the system. That's all it is. The system.

(They stare at each other. Blackout.)

End of Play

naked
faith

Ned Eisenberg and Dina Waters in *True To You*
Naked Angels at The Space in New York City (1995).

TRUE TO YOU
by Kenneth Lonergan

BIOGRAPHY

Kenneth Lonergan has been represented in New York by *Lobby Hero* (Playwrights Horizons, John Houseman Theatre, Drama Desk Best Play Nominee, Outer Critics Circle Best Play and John Gassner Playwrighting Nominee, included in the 2000-2001 Best Plays Annual), *The Waverly Gallery* (Williamstown Theatre Festival, Promenade; 2001 Pulitzer Prize Runner-up), and *This Is Our Youth* (Drama Desk Best Play Nominee). *Lobby Hero* (Olivier Award Nominee for Best Play) and *This Is Out Youth* have also received productions on London's West End. He co-wrote the film *Gangs of New York* which garnered a WGA and Academy Award nomination for Best Original Screenplay. His film *You Can Count On Me,* which he wrote and directed, was nominated for an Academy Award for Best Screenplay, won the Sundance 2000 Grand Jury Prize and The Waldo Salt Screenwriting Award, the NY Film Critics Circle, LA Films Critics Circle, Writers Guild of America and National Board of Review Awards for Best Screenplay of 2001, the AFI Awards for Best Film and Best New Writer, as well as the Sutherland Trophy at the London Film Festival. He is currently in post-production on his film *Margaret,* which he wrote and directed. He is a member of Naked Angels. He is married to actress J. Smith-Cameron.

ACKNOWLEDGMENTS

True To You was first produced by Naked Angels at The Space in New York City as a part of *Naked Faith* (February 8–25, 1995). It was directed by Gary Winick with the following cast:

MR. AUSTIN CARMODY .... Ned Eisenberg
SOPHIE .... Dina Waters

And the following production staff:

Set Design..Peter Harrison
Lighting Design .... Eric Thoben, Robert Perry
Costume Design .... Martha Bromelmeier
Sound Design...Roger Raines
Property Design.. Kristina Zill
Casting..Keli Lee

CAST OF CHARACTERS

AUSTIN CARMODY
SOPHIE, his secretary

SETTING

Mr. Carmody's lavish office.

TRUE TO YOU

A big, old-fashioned, lavish office. MR. AUSTIN CARMODY *is at his big desk. He is a stout, handsome business magnate of the 1920s type. He is reading some terrible documents. He hits his intercom.*

CARMODY. Sophie, could you come in here a minute please?

SOPHIE. *(On intercom:)* Yes Mr. Carmody.

(CARMODY gets up. SOPHIE, his trim little secretary comes in. [We employ the diminutive only for its evocation of the old fashioned flavor we wish to convey.])

SOPHIE. Yes Mr. Carmody?

CARMODY. Sit down, Sophie.

SOPHIE. Would you like some coffee, Mr. Carmody?

CARMODY. No thank you.

SOPHIE. Would you like a drink, Mr. Carmody?

CARMODY. No thank you, Sophie.

SOPHIE. It's after five, you know.

CARMODY. Yes, I know what time it is Sophie, but I don't care for anything just now, thank you.

SOPHIE. All right.

CARMODY. Sophie… How long have you been working for me?

SOPHIE. Five years.

CARMODY. Five years. And in that time, have you ever had any cause to complain of me?

SOPHIE. Oh no, Mr. Carmody. I think you're wonderful. Wonderful to work for, I mean, of course. Wonderful as an employer. A wonderful employer. All the staff thinks so.

CARMODY. Well— Thank you, Sophie.

SOPHIE. All the staff look up to you, Mr. Carmody.

CARMODY. Thank you Sophie, I certainly wish that were true.

SOPHIE. Oh it *is* true. The staff all worship you, Mr. Carmody, honestly they do, they *do*, Mr. Carmody.

CARMODY. I don't think Mr. Rosenfeld is too fond of me.

SOPHIE. Oh—well, Mr. Rosenfeld. He's— He's crazy. He walks around this office talking like a crazy man. Don't pay any attention to anything he says. Nobody else does.

CARMODY. Well, the Federal authorities seem to have been paying quite a lot of attention to what Mr. Rosenfeld has to say, I'm afraid Sophie. To the tune of twenty-seven separate indictments against me for tax fraud, insurance fraud, medical fraud and fraud.

SOPHIE. Well what do they know? They don't work here, they don't know you, they don't know what you do.

CARMODY. Well, I—

SOPHIE. They're crazy, those Federal authorities. They run around here trying to turn people against you, trying to turn the staff against you, they're a bunch of crazy men. I wouldn't pay any attention to what they say Mr. Carmody, I know no one on the staff does.

CARMODY. Well, if—

SOPHIE. They don't know the kind of man you are. You're wonderful.

CARMODY. Thank you Sophie. That kind of blind trust means a great deal to me at present, I can tell you that straight out.

SOPHIE. Oh Mr. Carmody.

CARMODY. But the thing of it is, Sophie, well, the thing is, these twenty-seven indictments they've got lined up against me, well, well the fact is, well the fact is Sophie they're turning out to be a bit of a problem.

SOPHIE. But surely not for *you,* Mr. Carmody? You haven't done anything wrong.

CARMODY. No, but I have to admit, I've got to face it, the whole situation is becoming a bit of a burden. A bit of a weight on the old back. You follow my meaning, my dear? A bit of a crippling weight on the old back. Why, just last night— This will give you an example of what I mean— Just last night, went home, told the wife about the twenty-seven indictments the government has lined up against me, and you know what she said? Eh? Take a guess, my dear, take a guess what my wife of fifteen years—picked her out of a window display at Macy's fifteen years ago, and introduced her to the world as Mrs. Austin Carmody—and guess what she had to say to me. Give you one guess.

SOPHIE. Oh, I can't guess…

CARMODY. She looked me in the eye and said "I don't know you."

SOPHIE. She went crazy.

CARMODY. "Austin," she said, "I don't know you." That's what she said to me, Sophie, and then she left the house.

SOPHIE. Oh Mr. Carmody.

CARMODY. Took my little twin daughters and left the house.

SOPHIE. Not the twins!

CARMODY. I'm afraid so. But the point is Sophie, I'm desperate. And frankly, you're the only person I can think of who really believes in me.

SOPHIE. Oh no, all the staff believe in you too.

CARMODY. Then why are they all testifying against me?

SOPHIE. I don't know.

CARMODY. Every single one!

SOPHIE. But they can't indict you for something you didn't do, can they?

CARMODY. Well, here's the thing, Sophie. These twenty-seven indictments are all of them complaints that the Federal Government is making against me, because I cannot find certain...records. Records containing the accounts of various people to whom this company has paid out millions of dollars over the years... And— This is the thing, the crazy thing: Thanks to the reckless fantasy of Burt Rosenfeld, the Federal Government of my own country—a government I had just a little bit to do with electing, thank you for asking—thinks that I...simply *invented* all these people, hundreds of clients, hundreds of beneficiaries, hundreds of claimants for medical insurance...so I could take all that money out of the company and funnel it into my own private numbered bank account in Switzerland.

SOPHIE. But that's ridiculous.

CARMODY. I know it. You know it. But damn it, how's a man supposed to vindicate himself when everybody's lined up against him?

SOPHIE. I'm not lined up against you Mr. Carmody.

CARMODY. I know that Sophie. And that's why the only person in the whole world who can help me now is you.

SOPHIE. Me?

CARMODY. Sophie—what you've got to do is, you've got to validate my story. You've got to swear under oath that *you* mislaid those files—there would be ten thousand of them in all—and you've got to go before the Grand Jury and confirm their existence and tell the judge you've mislaid them, lost them, left them on the bus, anything, for God's sake, only you've got to back me up or I'm going to go to jail, do you understand? Jail!

SOPHIE. But I never saw those files...

CARMODY. But you might have. You easily might have.

SOPHIE. Well I don't think it would be right for me to lie.

CARMODY. And is it right for them to lock me up in prison for the next ten years?

SOPHIE. No.

CARMODY. Are you worried about the consequences, Sophie? Is that it?

Worried about the repercussions? They'd never know. They'd never find out. And if they did you could always say I threatened your job if you didn't lie for me, something like that—

SOPHIE. Oh they'd never believe that.

CARMODY. For God's sake, woman, can you not see the hangman's noose swinging over my head! Somebody has got to help me or I won't be responsible for my actions! I'm absolutely desperate!

SOPHIE. Mr. Carmody I wish you wouldn't talk like that. You know I'd do almost anything for you. You know I think you're the most wonderful man in the world. You know it just kills me to see them hounding you like this, just because you lost some files. I don't understand any of this, Mr. Carmody. With so many really bad people in the world, so many really dishonest men, why do they have to pick on you? It seems so unfair. Maybe I could go to the authorities and explain to them how fair and honest and decent you are. How you always have a few minutes to talk to the staff and, and, how much I look up to you and how much I enjoy working for you...

CARMODY. Sophie, that's not going to work. The only thing that can save me now is if I can find one person to back me up, and well, if you won't help me, then I, I guess I'm finished.

(He sits down heavily.)

SOPHIE. I'll help you.

CARMODY. I'm sorry?

SOPHIE. I'll help you. I'd do anything for you, Mr. Carmody and that's the real truth.

CARMODY. Well I...I can't tell you how much that means to me, Sophie.

SOPHIE. What do you want me to say?

CARMODY. Well I...I want to you to memorize this list. These are the names of all the people documented in the missing files. And when they ask you if any of the names are familiar to you, I want you to say yes.

SOPHIE. That's not lying.

CARMODY. No... And then, when they ask you who the names on this list are, I want you to say that they are clients, beneficiaries, insurance claimants, that sort of thing.

SOPHIE. Well—aren't they?

CARMODY. Why, yes. Yes they are.

SOPHIE. Well that's not lying.

CARMODY. No it isn't. And then...when they ask if you have independent knowledge of the existence of these files, apart from my telling you about them—and if in fact you are entirely responsible for their disappearance—I want you to say yes.

SOPHIE. That would be lying.

CARMODY. That would be lying, yes.

SOPHIE. All right. I'll do it.

CARMODY. But the thing is Sophie… If you do this wonderful thing for me, there's no turning back. Because if you change your story midway through the proceedings, if you jump ship halfway through you could be sent to prison for a very long time. I wouldn't want that on my conscience.

SOPHIE. I won't jump ship.

CARMODY. Sophie…dear Sophie.

SOPHIE. Will that be all, Mr. Carmody?

CARMODY. Yes. No.

SOPHIE. Yes, Mr. Carmody?

CARMODY. Er— Tell me something about yourself, will you, my dear?

SOPHIE. What do you mean?

CARMODY. Well, it's been so long since I've talked to a friendly party…

SOPHIE. Oh, I know…

CARMODY. And, well we've, we've worked together, side by side as it were, for nearly five years… And here you are about to do this great thing for me at no inconsiderable risk to yourself, and I know very little about you, that's all.

SOPHIE. What do you want to know?

CARMODY. Well… Where do you live? Who are your friends? What do you do on the weekends? What are your hobbies? That kind of thing.

SOPHIE. Oh you wouldn't be interested in that.

CARMODY. Yes I would, Sophie, that isn't true.

SOPHIE. Well…I live in a little walk-up on Cornwall Street. My family are in Iowa. Sometimes one of the girls and I go to a movie on the weekend. I don't have many hobbies. No, that's not true, I like to play records. Sometimes I like to sit by the window on a Sunday afternoon and listen to the phonograph. Is that what you wanted to know?

CARMODY. Have you got a boyfriend?

SOPHIE. Oh no…

CARMODY. There must be somebody.

SOPHIE. I don't have time for a boyfriend. I work every day and on the weekends I'm so tired—

CARMODY. Aren't you ever lonely, Sophie?

SOPHIE. Yes.

CARMODY. Sophie…

SOPHIE. Yes, Austin? I mean yes Mr. Carmody?

(*He kisses her. A tender beautiful kiss on the mouth.*)

SOPHIE. I think I should go home now.

CARMODY. Yes, you're right.

SOPHIE. Will that be all, Mr. Carmody?

CARMODY. No Sophie.

(*She starts to go.*)

CARMODY. Sophie?

SOPHIE. Yes? Sir?

CARMODY. Why are you doing this for me?

SOPHIE. Because you're innocent.

(*He breaks down and sobs.*)

SOPHIE. Mr. Carmody. Oh Mr. Carmody please don't… Oh Mr. Carmody don't… You'll be sick…

CARMODY. I'm a wretch, a dirty wretch… Low, selfish…greedy…selfish…

SOPHIE. That's not true!

(*CARMODY gets ahold of himself.*)

CARMODY. Sophie, what would you say if I told you that in order to save my own neck I was willing to throw the only person that really believes in me into the teeth of the law and have them mash your life to jelly, on the absurdly slim chance they might swallow the ridiculous story I've asked you to tell them?

SOPHIE. I wouldn't believe you.

CARMODY. Why not?

SOPHIE. Because I don't think you would do that to me.

CARMODY. Sophie…what would you say if I told you that I am much, much guiltier than the authorities even suppose?

SOPHIE. I wouldn't believe that either.

CARMODY. For God's sake why not?

SOPHIE. Because I just can't imagine it.

CARMODY. What can you imagine, my dear?

SOPHIE. *(Enigmatically:)* Oh, I imagine a great deal in my little room, Mr. Carmody.

(Brief pause. She exits. Fade out.)

End of Play

A PASSION PLAY
by Pippin Parker

BIOGRAPHY

Pippin Parker is a founding member and former Artistic Director of Naked Angels and was Co-Artistic Director of the Democracy Issues Project.

As a writer, his plays include *Anesthesia, Assisted Living,* and an assortment of one acts, which have been produced in New York and Los Angeles. Television credits include the animated series *The Tick* and *Pocoyo.*

He was director and dramaturg of the original production of George Packer's *Betrayed* at Culture Project in New York (Lortel Award for Outstanding Play 2008), subsequently staged at The Kennedy Center in Washington, DC.

He is currently Chair of the graduate playwriting department at the New School for Drama (New School University) in New York and is a Writers Guild of America, East council member.

ACKNOWLEDGMENTS

A Passion Play was first produced by Naked Angels at The Space in New York City as a part of *Naked Faith* (February 8–25, 1995). It was directed by Frank Pugliese with the following cast:

NATALIE ....Missy Yager

DAVID... Patrick Breen

And the following production staff:

Set Design...Peter Harrison

Lighting Design .... Eric Thoben, Robert Perry

Costume Design ....Martha Bromelmeier

Sound Design...Roger Raines

Property Design.. Kristina Zill

Casting...Keli Lee

CAST OF CHARACTERS

NATALIE

DAVID

A PASSION PLAY

A small church somewhere in Europe. Light bleeds in through stained glass
windows above. There are no actual set pieces. The glass reliquary, the paint-
ings and frescoes are all suggested by the actors.

NATALIE enters. She has a sweater over her dress, a knapsack in her
hand.

NATALIE. Oh my God.

(She drops the knapsack. Looks around, overwhelmed.)

Oh my God, oh my God, oh my God, oh my God. *(Pause.) Oh* my God.
David. *(Turns back towards the door.)* David!

(DAVID enters, reading a thick guidebook, carrying a knapsack and a
larger bag. He looks up.)

DAVID. Wow.

NATALIE. Would you— Could you even believe this?

DAVID. Wow.

NATALIE. That's what I'm saying!

DAVID. I mean… Wow!

NATALIE. I know! Is this the most—

DAVID. Mmm-hmm.

NATALIE. The most beautiful— *(She gazes up.)* Oh! David!

DAVID. What?

NATALIE. The stained glass?

DAVID. Incredible.

NATALIE. No, but I mean the round— This little round one on top.

DAVID. Yes. The roseate. It's called a roseate. Beautiful.

NATALIE. This is— This *is*— Don't you think?

DAVID. Yeah.

NATALIE. I mean of *every*thing. Everywhere we've been.

(DAVID looks up, distracted.)

DAVID. Definitely. You think that's the original glass?

NATALIE. Oh, and these frescoes. And this *floor.* These *tiles* for Christ's
sake. *(She reaches down.)* Someone placed these in, one by one.

DAVID. *(Still looking up:)* Not much thousand-year-old glass left, you know.

NATALIE. *(Kneeling:)* None of these tiles are exactly the same. Look, David.

(DAVID gives them a quick glance.)

DAVID. Yes, they're all different. In their own incredibly similar way. *(Looking back up:)* Bet it's not the original glass *(DAVID thumbs through the guidebook.)*

NATALIE. But I mean, doesn't it just make you want to *cry*, or—or—

DAVID. *(Tapping the book:)* Thought so! Apparently the whole South wall was destroyed in the 14th century and then again in the late 1700s. There weren't even any windows on this side at *all* until 1958. You hear that, Natalie? Do I have the eye, or what?

    (NATALIE's on one knee.)

NATALIE. How do you genuflect. It's like this, right?

DAVID. What are you doing?

NATALIE. I had an impulse. You don't seem moved, you're not moved, are you moved?

DAVID. I *am*, it's just that you're *so* moved it's hard to match your level of… movement.

NATALIE. I could live here, couldn't you?

DAVID. *(Checking his watch:)* We may have to if we miss the train.

NATALIE. But couldn't you just stay here forever?

DAVID. Not without food. Hey, did you see that place?

NATALIE. No.

DAVID. With the tanks of eels and the tables out front?

NATALIE. *(Uninterested:)* Oh, yeah…

DAVID. Bet it's incredible. Because I don't know if you know this, but it's a local specialty. Eel.

NATALIE. I'm not hungry.

    (She moves to another wall.)

DAVID. I'm just saying, because there's no food on the train, you know. And you haven't eaten all day. I mean when's the last time you ate?

NATALIE. *(Shrugs.)* Wonder what this is?

DAVID. Huh, let's see what it says.

    (He comes over, opens the guidebook, reads. Lets out a little laugh.)

NATALIE. What?

DAVID. You'll never believe it. *(Reads:)* "The glass reliquary on the East wall displays a piece of the gown Mary is said to have been wearing when she gave birth to Jesus."

NATALIE. Really? That's incredible.

DAVID. Incredible, yeah, that'd be *one* word for it. Oh, and it says here there's *another* word for it.

NATALIE. What's that?

DAVID. Crock O'shit.

NATALIE. David.

DAVID. Oh, come on, Natalie. You really think this is real? You don't think maybe somewhere along the way the church might have had a little *attendance* problem? Maybe running low on the old *wine* fund?

NATALIE. David?

DAVID. Or no, some young priest is totally blowing his job interview, right, and he's like: "Oh, did I mention that I *own* a piece of the gown the *virgin* was wearing when she gave birth to a certain Lord of Lords? Did I forget to put that on my application?" No, you know what? I bet it was the *tile* man, who *sold* it to the priest, who *gave* it to the church—

NATALIE. David!

DAVID. What?

NATALIE. Well—it's just—it's a *church*, you know. Whatever.

(She walks away, studies another fresco.)

DAVID. *(Chastened:)* Okay, okay.

(They stand at opposite walls, backs to each other. DAVID starts to say something. Stops. Can't help himself:)

You know, I don't want to say anything, but they did burn down the library at Alexandria.

NATALIE. Who?

DAVID. The Christians.

NATALIE. Really.

DAVID. I mean it was only all the collected wisdom of the known world, that's all.

NATALIE. But fortunately, we have you.

DAVID. I mean if it hadn't been for them, we'd know a lot more. I mean we'd know how they built the *pyramids*.

NATALIE. Handy.

DAVID. Okay, but the point is, The Crusades, The Inquisition, they've committed the most gruesome, the bloodiest crimes in history and you have to keep that in perspective. Especially in a place like this. That's all I'm saying.

NATALIE. That's all you're saying?

DAVID. That's all I'm saying.

NATALIE. Good.

(She moves to another painting.)

DAVID. Although actually, it may have been *Caesar* who burned the library now that I think about it, but the point is— Well, you get my point.

(He looks back at her, crosses to her, looks at what she's looking at.)

That's nice.

(He looks in the book, then at the fresco, then back at the book.)

Catherine.

NATALIE. Hmmm…

DAVID. *(Reads:)* "Youngest of 25 children. As a girl she would kneel and say a Hail Mary on every step of the village as a sign of her devotion. At age 8, against her parents' wishes, she entered a convent where she lived in silence and solitude for 7 years, subsisting on nothing but one orange every other day." One big orange.

(He looks to NATALIE, who's studying the painting.)

DAVID. *(Reading:)* "After her religious seclusion, she dedicated her life to the care of the poor and the sick, yaddah, yaddah… At 28— Oh, this is good— At 28, in an ecstatic rapture, her hands were pierced by five blood red rays, which were visible even after her death at age 33."

NATALIE. Thirty-three…

DAVID. Yep. You better get busy.

NATALIE. I know.

(She's still staring at the portrait. DAVID points to another painting, trying to draw her attention away.)

DAVID. Hey, what's that?

NATALIE. I don't know.

DAVID. Looks like pliers or something.

(He thumbs through the book again.)

NATALIE. Gonna look it up in your little book?

DAVID. Maybe. Okay. "St. Apollonia. 3rd century deaconess of the church persecuted by a magician who was held in great esteem by the pagan population—"

NATALIE. Magician?

DAVID. Uh-huh. "Awaited her martyrdom with joy, preaching the faith—"

NATALIE. That's weird.

DAVID. What?

NATALIE. Magicians and saints?

DAVID. I know, such a fine distinction, right? How did they ever tell them apart?

NATALIE. I think the saints were thinner. On the average.

DAVID. Probably. "As punishment, she was bound to a column and her teeth were pulled out by pincers." *(He looks at the painting again.)* Oh yeah, that's what they are. I was close. Again, the eye. "Often pictured with a pair of pincers holding a tooth… *(He laughs:)* She is the patron saint of dentists!"

NATALIE. It doesn't say that.

DAVID. Yes. It's right here.

NATALIE. Give me that.

(She grabs the book from his hands.)

DAVID. Ouch. Hey, watch the fingernails.

(She reads, he leans over her shoulder, points.)

See? Patron saint of dentists. Right there in black and white. Didn't believe me, huh?

NATALIE. I have an idea. How about we not consult any books for like five minutes. You think that's possible?

DAVID. Sure.

(NATALIE goes back to the portrait of Catherine. DAVID roams the room, looks at his watch.)

DAVID. Actually, we don't even really *have* five minutes. I mean if we're going to eat.

(She doesn't respond.)

Don't you want to eat? *(Pause.)* I have a real *feeling* about that place. Like it could be a very important discovery for us.

NATALIE. *(Calm:)* I wonder why you're so obsessed with finding these goddamned little restaurants all over the place.

DAVID. I'm not *obsessed*—

NATALIE. Yes. Everywhere we go it's like where's the *real* food? Where do the *real* people eat? Let's walk *around* for six or seven hours so we can survey every eating establishment in the *province.*

DAVID. It's just our last meal and I don't want to eat around the airport because it's all just—

NATALIE. God forbid you should have a dish that isn't one hundred percent authentic. God forbid some poor restauranteur tries to pull one *over* on you.

DAVID. No, but there's a finite number of meals, and I don't want to *waste* any.

NATALIE. Okay, okay, it's just— I miss it. We haven't even left and I already miss it. Wouldn't you love to come here all the time. I mean like every week.

DAVID. Sure, except we live eight *thousand* miles away and we're not Catholic.

NATALIE. I know. We're not anything.

DAVID. What do you mean? We're New Yorkers.

NATALIE. I mean did you ever go to church? I never did.

DAVID. Sure, I went to church. I went to church, I went to temple, when Dad married Chloe we all went to an Ashram. I hosted a Bhai dinner once.

NATALIE. It's no *wonder* we're so confused.

DAVID. Well I'm not confused. I'm not. And I don't think what religion our parents are has any importance at all because the truth is the whole meaning of religion has just been gutted, you know. Totally gutted. I mean you read whatever, Matthew, the book of Matthew, and you think, geez, some pretty good ideas here, something to shoot for, but over time anything worthy, anything of substance, has been systematically removed. And now all that's left is this really attractive shell. Very beautiful, totally hollow. And you know what? I'm really getting hungry.

NATALIE. I have to say, you can spend your whole life looking for all these contradictions, but ultimately, *ultimately,* you have to believe in something bigger.

DAVID. Listen, I have a hard enough time believing in myself, okay?

NATALIE. I know, but you end up reducing the whole world to a series of facts and there's no room for anything else.

DAVID. Well what do you want me to do. Convert?

NATALIE. No. I think we should stay.

DAVID. Sure, that'd be great, but—

NATALIE. *(Excited:)* Let's stay. Come on. Why not?

DAVID. Because we can't. Because we have things to—

      *(*NATALIE *pulls away.)*

NATALIE. See? See? Nobody stays. Everyone *says* they want to, but nobody does. Because it's too scary. So they find a thousand reasons for not going back. But it doesn't have to be, it doesn't. *(She points to the portrait.)* I mean you look at her, and you can make fun and say it never happened, she never lived in silence or had all those brothers and sisters, but she had something, a *purpose*, so what's fear compared to that? And I don't think she would have gone back, you know, if she were me, because what's the point? Why? What's to go back for? An overpriced apartment and a meaningless career and the telephone calls and voice mail and credit cards and getting disgusting food delivered every ten minutes and newer computers and six thousand flavors of coffee and no purpose to anything just running around in a panic hoping to elude that feeling you know is there, you know, that feeling that you're just floating in an empty sea and pretty soon you're one of those *people* going to certain *stores* to buy rocks and all that angel crap, or those recordings with the bad music and guidance because you're right, it *has* been gutted, nothing has any meaning, but I can't live like that anymore and I know it's just one tiny stupid hope against a thousand good reasons but why not stay. Why not? Why not? We could do it.

(She opens her fists which have been clenched so hard that her fingernails have drawn blood. She reaches into her knapsack.)

I have an orange. We could stay.

(DAVID comes over. Takes the orange. Looks at it. At her hands.)

DAVID. I read somewhere, that in the middle ages, if someone said they had a—a—vision, or a message, from God or whatever, no one would have thought to question it. To wonder whether it was real, or imagined. It didn't make any difference to them. Because it was still a sign. It still had meaning.

(He looks at her. Tries to think of something to say.)

(Lights.)

End of Play

naked
and
hate free

Bradley White in *Shadow Day*
Naked Angels at Theater 3 in New York City (1996).

SHADOW DAY
by Steven Dietz

BIOGRAPHY

Mr. Dietz's thirty-plus plays have been produced at regional theatres across the United States, as well as Off-Broadway. International productions of his work have been seen in England, Japan, Germany, France, Australia, Sweden, Russia, Slovenia, Argentina, Peru, Greece, Singapore, and South Africa. Recent plays include *Fiction* (produced Off-Broadway by the Roundabout Theatre Company); the Pulitzer-nominated *Last of the Boys* (produced by Steppenwolf Theatre, Chicago); and several widely-produced adaptations: *Honus and Me* (from Dan Gutman), and the Edgar Award-winning *Sherlock Holmes: The Final Adventure* (from William Gillette and Arthur Conan Doyle). Other plays include *Inventing van Gogh, The Nina Variations, Private Eyes, Halcyon Days, God's Country,* and *Lonely Planet* (PEN-USA Award for Drama). Mr. Dietz's work as a director has been seen at many of America's leading regional theatres. He divides his time between Seattle and Austin, where he is a professor at the University of Texas.

ACKNOWLEDGMENTS

Shadow Day was first produced by Naked Angels at Theater 3 in New York City as a part of *Naked and Hate Free* (July–August, 1996). It was directed by Joe Brancato with the following cast:

DANNY MACK ....Bradley White
KIMBERLY..Kharisma Gooden

And the following production staff:

Producer... Geoffrey Nauffts
Set Design..George Xenos
Lighting Design ....Shawn P. Gallagher, James Vermeulen
Sound Design...Rob Gould
Stage Manager...Meredith Bergman

CAST OF CHARACTERS

DANNY MACK, radio talk-show host
KIMBERLY, a fifth-grader

Amplified, offstage voices:
CALLER
NEW CALLER
BRIAN'S VOICE

TIME AND PLACE

The present.
A large American city.

SETTING

A radio studio.

SHADOW DAY

DANNY *at his microphone. The "ON THE AIR" sign is on.*

DANNY. You're what—you're twenty—you think somebody owes you a—

CALLER. *(Voice of a young man:)* I don't think anybody owes me anything, but I—

DANNY. Well, hey, *cop to this*—as they'd say in the finer neighborhoods— your Mother is gone, Troy. You and the rest of your ilk have been sucking off the teet of Mother America since JFK was downing pills and bedding starlets. So, what you've got to—

CALLER. You don't even know me—you are totally out of line making a—

DANNY. *I'm* out of line? Get a grip my little twenty-something *leech.* You've been raised on Mama's food stamps and welfare and now the bills have come due and you've got nothing to *contribute.* You're a shell. You're the *host body* for government waste. What can you do? What can any of you do? Walk the talk, steal sneakers and peddle crack? We don't need you, Troy. You're surplus, you're urban landfill.

CALLER. How can you—I'm not a criminal. I was never in a gang—do you see how you—I'm a sophomore at Georgetown and I—

DANNY. What were your SATs?

CALLER. What?

DANNY. What were your scores? What percentile were you in? You don't know and WHY: because I'd bet the farm you're a charity case, Troy. You're a QUOTA, my friend. Your skin got you in to where your scores could not. Am I right? You've grown silent, Mr. Sophomore—

CALLER. You can't—you—you—

DANNY. And your verbal skills are nothing to speak of, either—

CALLER. You don't even have the guts to answer my question—

DANNY. Your question, Troy, was "Shouldn't society care for those who are economically disadvantaged?" Am I right? Was that your question?

CALLER. Yes, and if you—

DANNY. Well, let me make it simple for you, Troy. The answer is "No." And WHY: Because a society is a set of rules. Drive on this side of the street. Exchange this green paper for goods and services. Fight the wars, finance the schools, select your representatives. Water will come out of the tap, someone will pick up your garbage, there will be bread on the shelves and gas for your car. These are the rules of the game. And if you are *unsuc-cessful* at the game—if what you have to offer as a skill is not in *demand*—YOU WILL NOT DO WELL. You will go hungry and sleep in your own vomit and people will walk past you and laugh at your tattered little face and WHY: because they took on the same rules as you and THEY WON. They've got a beer in their hand and a dish on the roof—AND NOBODY GAVE IT TO THEM. It was not a *handout,* Troy, it didn't come down from the back of a truck like government cheese, it was—

CALLER. You can't—you do not have the—

DANNY. And nowhere in this pact is anything that says: Oh, by the way, after you've EARNED your goods and securities, GIVE IT BACK—let it be bled from you so that someone WHO IS A FAILURE—and you are a failure, Troy—SO SOMEONE LIKE TROY CAN SIT ON HIS ASS AND LET MOTHER AMERICA BRING HIM EVERYTHING HE NEEDS.

CALLER. You *[bleeeeeeep]*—you're a *[bleeeeeeep]*—

(*DANNY clicks the CALLER off.*)

DANNY. This is what becomes of them. They resort to profanity. The liberal leeches in this great land will tax your every breath and give your last dime to a lesbian crack addict—but when they are forced to ARTIC-ULATE THEIR BELIEFS—*not* their FEARS, *not* their PITY, *not* their *FEELINGS*—but their BELIEFS…they have nothing to say.

Never have so many been so silent in the face of true opposition.

(*A look up at a clock.*)

It's one fifty-nine. This is Danny Mack. Stay tuned.

(*A bit of music up, then it fades down and out. DANNY sips from a bottle of mineral water. Looks through some papers near him. Holds one up, and he talks to his [unseen] engineer in the [offstage] control booth.*)

Is this for real, Brian?

(*Smile.*)

You're kidding?

(*Listens.*)

All across the city?

(*Listens.*)

Perfect. You're the best, I've told you—

(*Stops.*)

What?

(*Laughs.*)

Yeah, right.

(Quick sip of mineral water. Back on the air.)

It's two p.m. I'm Danny Mack. Deal with it. Now, before we go to your calls, I would be remiss to not mention this little gem that Brian, my engineer, has unearthed. It seems they've found another creative use for your tax dollars, my friends. As we know, they are no longer content to build your roads badly, deliver your mail late and give grants to pornographers—no—they've outdone themselves this time. Check it out:

Today, in businesses across this city, today is "Shadow Day." This means they're hauling select fifth and sixth graders out of public school—where they're busy being taught that Columbus raped the Indians and the Founding Fathers were all evil white slave masters—they're hauling them, at your expense, *with your tax dollars,* out of school and busing them around the city. The kid then spends the day "shadowing" an adult—following them around all day, supposedly learning about a given profession…when, point of fact, all they'll learn is how well adults can lie to children.

Who thinks up this malarkey?! This is education?! This is the best we can do?! Just plop 'em in an office and say "Here, this is what you have to look forward to"? And at taxpayer expense too. What ever happened to that time-honored-but-much-in-disfavor tactic of *actually teaching them?!*

I mean, hey, it's not the kids fault. Hell, they'll take a day away from school and laugh all the way to the mall. And some of 'em will end up on the "cute sign-off story" of the local evening news. But this is yet another example of the soft-skinned, politically correct education system in this country that would much rather think up "interesting models of schooling" than deal with the hard realities of illiteracy, teenage pregnancy and gang violence. And WHY: just as I said before—they have feelings which they mistake for *thoughts.* They feel bad about a poor kid in the projects and having had this feeling they think they've had an idea. But since they can't articulate it, they *cushion* it, they *protect* it. They build a society which gives comfort to the things in the world which make them feel bad. They build a world which will assuage their guilt. This is not governance, this is therapy.

I'd like to see them try that with me. I'd like to see them try to send one of these kids in here in the name of "education," in the name of "progressive thought." You want to know a progressive thought: get all the Mexican kids to speak English. This is our native tongue—learn it or leave. You want another progressive though: make all these teenage girls have babies in the school cafeteria with no doctors to help 'em—and let the other girls watch and learn the joyous outcome of teenage sex. You want to *legislate feelings,* fine, here's another one: kid brings a gun to school, have him shoot his finger off. No, really. Let's see how tough he is—take him outside, have him hold the gun to the little finger of his other hand and pull the trigger—let's see if he's Mr. Tough Talk now, let's see if he knows how violence *feels*.

But no—their plan is to send little girls following after secretaries, finding out what kind of pantyhose they wear and how much the boss drinks at the Christmas party. Give me a break. I promise you, if they tried to pull that stunt on me, I'd—

> *(He stops. He looks up—Standing in the room is a ten-year-old black girl. She wears jeans and a sweatshirt. Nikes on her feet. She carries a backpack. Her name is KIMBERLY.*
>
> *DANNY stares at her, but speaks to his [unseen] engineer.)*

Brian?

> *(No answer.)*

Brian, what is this?

> *(Still no answer.)*

Brian, I think I've found something for the lost and found.

> *(Pause, then a quick laugh.)*

Okay, you've had your fun—but we've got callers on the line and I'm not in the mood for—

> *(Silence. He pushes some buttons, looks around. The "ON THE AIR" sign is now off.)*

Hey, c'mon. I know you can hear me. Are we still on the air? I'll have your ass, do you hear me? What is this girl doing in here? Are we on the air or not? Brian—

> *(Long silence. Finally, he turns to KIMBERLY.)*

Hi.

> *(She stares at him.)*

What can I do for you?

> *(She stares at him, giving no response.)*

Oh, of course, they've covered all the bases—you're *deaf* too. Perfect.

> *(He stands.)*

Look, I don't know why you're here, but why don't you—

> *(She hands him a piece of paper. He looks at it. Then, takes it from her. Reads, quickly:)*

Great. You're my shadow.

> *(Her first reaction: a beautiful, warm smile.)*

Isn't that cute. Excuse me for a moment.

(He sits back down, talks into his mic:)

Well, we've had a little studio excitement here. Some jokers on our staff let an innocent little black girl into our midst. So, let me take this opportunity to—

(Stops. Looks at the table in front of him. Touches a few buttons.)

Brian, are we on?

(Pause.)

Test, one, two—

(Taps the mic.)

What the hell are—

(Stops. Sits. Fumes. Suddenly stands and begins to storm out of the room—)

BRIAN—

NEW CALLER. *(Voice of an older man, with a quiet, raspy laugh:)* Brian's gone, Danny. And don't try the door, it's locked.

(A light shift in the room. DANNY squints, trying to see into the control room.)

DANNY. Who the hell are—turn the lights on in there—RIGHT NOW— and put me back on the air—

(Goes to a phone on his console.)

I don't know who you are or what you want, but security is gonna have your ass on a platter, pal, so if I were you I'd—

(Hearing that the phone line is dead, he clicks the receiver a few times, then hurls the phone down.)

Okay. Enough. What's your game? You've got an innocent little girl in here, so watch yourself. You got something to tell me, tell me. I'm used to dealing with nutcakes, but you've got a kid in here who's—

NEW CALLER. Who's innocent.

DANNY. Yes. Who's—

NEW CALLER. I don't think so, Danny.

DANNY. What are you taking ab—

NEW CALLER. Her name is Kimberly. And she's brought you a present.

(Silence. DANNY looks at KIMBERLY. She stares at him, warmly.)

Haven't you, Kimberly?

KIMBERLY. Yes.

NEW CALLER. A little gift for our friend, Danny Mack. It's in your backpack, isn't it, Kimberly?

KIMBERLY. Yes.

NEW CALLER. I bet Danny wants to see it, don't you, Danny?

(DANNY plops back down in his chair.)

DANNY. God, I could still be a weatherman in Omaha. Get up, pull the info off the wire, pick out a tie, stand up there in front of my map. Look, Kimberly, Mr. Deep Throat. I'm tired of this. I got a listenership of four million people—most, if not all, of whom are calling this station, calling the cops, calling the National Guard for godsakes to find out what's going on—not for my safety, you see, but for theirs. They don't get their hit of brutal humor and well-placed hate, it wrecks their day. So, you've had your fun, let's just—

NEW CALLER. No, Danny. We haven't had our fun. Not yet. Have we, Kimberly?

(KIMBERLY shakes her head "No.")

It's Shadow Day, Danny. And Kimberly, with our help, has shadowed you. She knows where you live—though you didn't sleep at home last night, your wife being out of town and that flight attendant being so willing. We had a window seat, Danny. Kimberly knows your car, your private parking spot, the name of the guard, the name of the station manager, the name of your engineer—all of whom were very helpful. They all paid close attention.

DANNY. Hey, I don't know what sort of dementia you're dealing with, but—

NEW CALLER. I'm not dealing with dementia. I'm dealing with an assault rifle. It's the real reason everyone was so kind to us. Polite, even.

DANNY. Look, you're sick, you need help and I don't—

NEW CALLER. Shut. The Fuck. Up. Danny.

(Silence.)

It's Shadow Day and Kimberly has a little gift for you. Don't you, Kimberly?

KIMBERLY. Yes.

DANNY. What the –

NEW CALLER. Sit down, Danny. I've got your bloodless heart in my scope. So, sit. *Now.*

(DANNY looks at the glass, looks at KIMBERLY…then sits.)

Thank you. Now, please, Kimberly, why don't you show us what you brought to the station?

(KIMBERLY walks up to the console, near DANNY. As she begins to

slowly unzip her backpack. . .we begin to hear. . .ticking. Faint, at first. Then growing a bit louder. When the backpack is fully unzipped, she very carefully reaches inside—

DANNY *watches her, frozen, motionless.*

From inside the backpack, KIMBERLY *removes an old, weathered cigar box. The ticking continues. She sets the box directly in from of* DANNY.)

Go ahead, now, Kimberly. Don't be afraid. Open it. Open it up and show Danny what you've brought.

*(*KIMBERLY *stares at* DANNY *for a moment. He speaks to her.)*

DANNY. Kimberly, listen, you don't have to do this—

KIMBERLY. *(Calmly:)* I know. But I want to.

*(*KIMBERLY *begins to open the box. The ticking grows louder.)*

DANNY. BRIAN, CALL THE POLICE—

NEW CALLER. I'm afraid you're on your own, big man. No one is coming to help you. Isn't that what you always wanted—*less government intervention?* Well, here you are.

*(*KIMBERLY *opens the box, slowly—as* DANNY *holds tight to the arms of his chair. Ticking grows still louder.*

She reaches into the box and brings out. . .a crumpled piece of paper.

She unfolds the paper.

She leans in toward Danny's microphone.

She clears her throat, softly.

The "ON THE AIR" sign goes on.)

KIMBERLY. *(Into the mic, reading from the paper, simply, calmly:)* "Everything that we see is a shadow cast by that which we do not see. Every riot is the language of those unheard."

(Silence. KIMBERLY *folds the paper and puts it back in the box.)*

NEW CALLER. We've brought you Dr. King's words, Danny.

*(*DANNY *just stares front.)*

As well as one final word.

*(*KIMBERLY *reaches, again, into the cigar box. This time she brings out. . . an alarm clock, still ticking loudly.*

She sets it on the console in front of DANNY. *She looks at him. Then, she leans close to the microphone and says, simply. . .)*

KIMBERLY. Bang.

(The "ON THE AIR" sign goes off, as—

KIMBERLY *turns to him and smiles, warmly. She leaves the clock tick-*

ing on his console. She puts the cigar box back in her backpack, zips it up, straps it to her back, turns and heads out. Before she is gone, she turns back to him…and waves goodbye with her fingers. Then, she is gone.

DANNY *sits, motionless. The clock continues to tick, loudly. Suddenly, the alarm on the clock goes off, loud and obnoxious—*

DANNY *slams the clock, violently, shutting the alarm off, as—*

Lights return to normal and—

The "ON THE AIR" sign goes back on.)

BRIAN'S VOICE. Danny. Danny, you okay? You're on the air, pal. We're waiting.

(DANNY looks in the direction of Brian. He looks at his mic.)

Danny?

(Silence. He leans in close to his mic. Speaks slowly, cautiously.)

DANNY. *(Gradually getting up to speed as he talks:)* No. I'd love it. I really would. I'd love to see 'em send one of those kids in here. I'd have 'em sit down and write their congressman a letter—or, better yet, I'd march 'em down to city hall and show those bonehead low-lifes where their Great Society has gotten us. It's gotten us to this place, and it's time to tell our people the truth, because they deserve the truth and they can handle the truth and the truth shall set them—

KIMBERLY'S VOICE. Bang.

(Silence. He looks up at a clock. He continues.)

DANNY. It's two p.m. I'm Danny Mack. Deal with it. Listen, the hard fact of the matter is that *liberty and charity do not mix.* If you want one, you say goodbye to the other. If you want to do good for everyone, fine—but you say goodbye to liberty. And if you want to grant people their freedom, true freedom to build any life they can—you can flush away your charity. You can't have both. You give it or you get it. It's that—

KIMBERLY'S VOICE. Bang.

DANNY. It's that—

KIMBERLY'S VOICE. Bang.

DANNY. It's that simple.

(Fast blackout.)

End of Play

BABY STEPS
by Geoffrey Nauffts

BIOGRAPHY

Geoffrey Nauffts has worked as an actor both on and off Broadway, regionally and extensively in film and television. He has directed short plays by Kenneth Lonergan, Frank Pugliese, David Marshall Grant, Theresa Rebeck and Suzan-Lori Parks, as well as the critically acclaimed production of Steven Belber's *Tape* in New York, Los Angeles and London. He wrote, directed and co-starred in the award-winning short film *Baby Steps* with Kathy Bates and co-wrote *Jenifer,* a movie of the week for CBS with David Marshall Grant. He and Anthony Barrile are currently collaborating with Elton John on a score for *Showstopper,* a screenplay they wrote for Ben Stiller's company, Red Hour. His critically acclaimed play *Next Fall* (winner of the 2008 Theater Visions Fund Award from the Blanche and Irving Laurie Foundation) played to packed houses in an extended run at the Peter Jay Sharp theater. He is the current artistic director of Naked Angels where he's been a proud member for over twenty-three years.

ACKNOWLEDGMENTS

Baby Steps was first produced by Naked Angels at Theater 3 in New York City as a part of *Naked and Hate Free* (July–August, 1996). It was directed by Michael Mastro with the following cast:

ROSEMARY	Marceline Hugot
ROBERT	Geoffrey Nauffts

And the following production staff:

Producer	Geoffrey Nauffts
Set Design	George Xenos
Lighting Design	Shawn P. Gallagher, James Vermeulen
Sound Design	Rob Gould

CAST OF CHARACTERS

ROSEMARY
ROBERT

BABY STEPS

An office. Clean and tidy. A shaft of late afternoon light pours through a window onto a half-dead potted plant that rests on and an old, oak the desk. ROSEMARY MELON, 40s, sits behind the desk, talking on the phone. The other line starts to ring.

ROBERT KAHN, 30s, stands awkwardly in the middle of the room, unclear as to whether he should sit or not. His tie seems to strangle him with every breath.

ROSEMARY. I'm sorry, but it's out of the question... No, I never said that *(To her secretary in the outer office:)* Maria?! *(Back into the phone:)* No, I didn't...

(Gesturing to ROBERT:)

Please. Have a seat. *(To the secretary:)* Maria? Would you get the other line, please!! *(Not getting any response, she goes back to the phone:)* Hold on.

(ROBERT sits, gingerly. ROSEMARY clicks over to the other line.)

Great Lakes Adoption Agency... Oh, hi! Can I call you back in a half hour?... Great.

(She clicks back to the other line.)

Listen, it's not going to happen, sweetie... Because you already have one... Yes, you do. You have a baby... I'm not going to discuss this with you right now. There's someone in my...

(She rolls her eyes at ROBERT and makes a yapping motion with her fingers.)

You deserve another one?... Oh, you do, do you? Well, I'm not so sure about that... Because you already have one... No, I'm not having a cow, I just don't feel like discussing this right now.

(She smiles at ROBERT, hanging herself with an imaginary noose.)

I know it's not a Baby Cuddles... Look, I'm not talking about this anymore... Because I said so... Ask your father... I'm hanging up now... Yes, I am... Okay... We'll see... Uh-huh... I love you too... Bye-bye.

(She hangs up, collapsing on the phone.)

I'm so sorry Mr...

ROBERT. Kahn. Robert Kahn.

ROSEMARY. Mr. Kahn. Please, forgive me.

ROBERT. No, I totally understand. Your daughter sounds just like my niece. All she wanted was a Baby Cuddles for her birthday. I went to like eight different toy stores before I finally found one... Had to wrestle a little old lady to the ground, but...

(ROSEMARY starts leafing through files on her desk.)

ROBERT. I love kids.

ROSEMARY. Well, you can't always get what you want.

ROBERT. That's true.

(She can't seem to find what she's looking for.)

I was kidding, by the way. I didn't actually wrestle an old lady to the ground.

ROSEMARY. I'm sure you didn't.

(ROBERT picks a brown leaf off her potted plant.)

Oh, the poor thing. I'm such a neglectful parent. I'm afraid I don't have much of a green thumb.

ROBERT. Just needs a little water.

(She bends over and sifts through more files on the floor.)

ROSEMARY. Kahn... Kahn... I seem to have misplaced your preliminary questionnaire.

ROBERT. I never got one.

(She pops back up.)

ROSEMARY. You never... Huh... My secretary was supposed to have sent you one so you could mail it back before we... Oh well, she's on maternity leave of all things, and this new girl, Maria, well, let's just say things have gotten a little screwy around here... Not to worry, we'll just... Why don't we... Why don't you tell me a little about yourself.

(ROSEMARY opens a note pad.)

Married?

ROBERT. Excuse me?

ROSEMARY. Are you married? I notice you're not wearing a wedding ring. Some people prefer not to. My husband, for instance. Makes his finger swell up like a carrot. Hasn't worn one in years. Bad circulation, I guess.

(ROBERT smiles, awkwardly.)

So, how about it, Mr. Kahn?

ROBERT. Huh?

ROSEMARY. How's your circulation?

ROBERT. Oh, yes... Sorry... You'll have to forgive me, Mrs. Melons. I'm usually a lot quicker. It's just—

ROSEMARY. —Melon.

ROBERT. I'm sorry?

ROSEMARY. It's one Melon not two.

ROBERT. Melon… Yes, of course. I'm sorry… Mrs. Melon. *(He makes a joke:)* I must be hungry. *(She doesn't get it.)* What was the question?

ROSEMARY. Are… You…

ROBERT. Married… Yes… Right.

    (She jots something down in the note pad.)

No… I mean, no, I'm not. That would be a "no" to that question.

    (She crosses his previous answer out. ROBERT *watches, intently.)*

ROBERT. Is…

ROSEMARY. Yes?

ROBERT. Is that a bad thing?

ROSEMARY. Is it a bad thing?

ROBERT. Yes… In the…uh…in the scheme of things. Is it, you know, would that be considered a bad thing?

    *(*ROSEMARY *closes the note pad and stares at him.)*

ROSEMARY. Why don't you tell me what it is you want, Mr. Kahn.

ROBERT. What I want?

ROSEMARY. Yes. What you're here for.

ROBERT. Okay. Well… I'm interested in adopting a child, I suppose.

ROSEMARY. You suppose?

ROBERT. Well, yes. You know. "I suppose." It's a figure of speech. I… It doesn't sound very…um… Okay… I'm here to inquire about adopting a kid. A child. I want to… I would like very much to adopt a child.

ROSEMARY. And what does that mean to you?

ROBERT. What does it mean to me?

ROSEMARY. Yes.

ROBERT. Like in a…

ROSEMARY. What does it mean to you, Mr. Kahn? To adopt a child. The idea of adopting a child.

ROBERT. Well, I supp… I mean… It means…taking care of someone?… Um… Teaching… Nurturing…… Loving…

    *(*ROSEMARY *opens the pad and starts taking notes again.* ROBERT *tries to sneak a peak at what she's writing. She covers the pad so he can't see.)*

Supporting…um… Total acceptance… *(Relieved that he's finally landed on what he thinks she'll think the right answer is:)* Unconditional love.

ROSEMARY. And what else?

ROBERT. What else?

ROSEMARY. Yes. Is there anything else?

ROBERT. Well... Hmm... I think that's... Off hand, I'd have to say that's... a lot, really.

ROSEMARY. Yes it is.

ROBERT. Pfew!

ROSEMARY. But is there anything else?

ROBERT. *(Beginning to flop sweat:)* Oh, boy! I feel like I'm missing something. Like I'm being tested or something.

ROSEMARY. There are no rights or wrongs, Mr. Kahn. I just want to give you the opportunity to say whatever's on your mind.

ROBERT. I see... Well, I think that's it for that one... Next.

ROSEMARY. What do you do for a living?

ROBERT. I'm a teacher. Jr. High school. Mostly English, but I've taught all subjects. Except for gym and art. I'm not much for either, really.

(She jots that down.)

Not that I don't like sports. Or art for that matter. It's just... I just...

(ROSEMARY stifles a yawn.)

I'm an English teacher...Jr. High.

ROSEMARY. Thank you.

ROBERT. And I volunteer at a deaf grade school. I'm learning sign language, so I volunteer. I hope to...one day soon...teach at an all deaf high school.

ROSEMARY. I see.

ROBERT. I prefer older kids... Teaching older kids... I just like to know what I'm...that I'm getting through, you know? Some people say it's harder, but I don't think so... I prefer it.

(ROSEMARY pulls a loose thread from her sweater.)

Blah. Blah. Blah. I'm rambling, aren't I? Oy.

ROSEMARY. Jewish?

ROBERT. Um... Sort of... I mean, I have no religion, really. My mother was Jewish. I was circumcised. That's about it. Why? Is... Is that...

(He refers to her note pad.)

ROSEMARY. It's fine, Mr. Kahn. It wasn't actually a question. It was more of an observation.

ROBERT. Oh, I see... Well, good observation.

(He loosens the tie around his neck.)

ROSEMARY. Would you care for some water?

ROBERT. Please.

(She pours them each a glass and resumes note taking.)

ROSEMARY. Why don't you tell me a little bit about your relationships, Mr. Kahn?

ROBERT. Really?

ROSEMARY. Really. We going to need to know about your personal life. You say you're not married. Are you seeing anyone?

ROBERT. We're going to get into all of that right now?

ROSEMARY. Now or later, Mr. Kahn. We're going to have to delve into aspects of your life that are very, well…private, but unfortunately—

ROBERT. —Yes. No, yes. Of course. I understand.

ROSEMARY. So… Are you currently in a relationship?

ROBERT. No… No relationship… I'm single.

(She jots that down.)

ROSEMARY. Have you ever been married?

ROBERT. Nope.

ROSEMARY. How about a long term relationship? Have you ever been in one of those?

ROBERT. Um…yes. I have actually.

ROSEMARY. How long?

ROBERT. Ten years.

ROSEMARY. Oh… And was there ever talk of children during that time, or is this a new desire?

ROBERT. Oh, no. There was always talk of children. Not as much on my part as theirs…initially… Well, I guess that's not true… We always wanted children… Both of us.

ROSEMARY. Uh-huh. And what happened?

ROBERT. We never…you know…had any.

ROSEMARY. And why was that?

(ROBERT shifts uncomfortably in his chair.)

ROBERT. He died.

ROSEMARY. Excuse me?

ROBERT. My partner… He died… And therefore the relationship ended, and we never had children.

(ROSEMARY's speechless.)

He's been gone for a little over a year now, and the desire to raise a child, if anything, it's gotten worse.

ROSEMARY. I'm sorry for your friend, Mr.…Robert… May I call you

Robert?

ROBERT. Please.

ROSEMARY. AIDS, I presume?

ROBERT. Yes, actually.

ROSEMARY. Insidious disease… I wouldn't wish it on anyone.

ROBERT. No…

(She looks at him, sympathetically.)

I'm fine, by the way. I mean… I'm negative.

ROSEMARY. Thank God.

ROBERT. Yeah…

(She closes her note pad.)

ROSEMARY. Listen, I think that's all we need to do today. Why don't you just fill out this questionnaire on your own time, mail it back and we'll take it from there.

(She hands him the blank form and rises.)

It was very nice to meet you, Robert. And I apologize for the confusion with my secretary and all.

ROBERT. Not at all.

(He takes the form, shakes her hand and starts off. ROSEMARY *sits back down and gets to work. Unable to leave,* ROBERT *stops and turns.)*

ROBERT. It's bad isn't it?

ROSEMARY. Hm?

ROBERT. All of it. My whole demographic. It's not doable.

ROSEMARY. Now, Robert, there are a lot of factors that figure into the adoption process. We've only just begun.

ROBERT. Yes, but then why do I feel like it's over?

ROSEMARY. I don't know. Why do you?

ROBERT. Because it's not right. Because I'm not fit. Because you feel I'm not fit.

ROSEMARY. I never said that.

ROBERT. Yes, but you feel it. You'll continue the charade for a while. Let me fill out your little questionnaire. But you probably won't even read it.

ROSEMARY. Now, Mr. Kahn, I think you're being a bit over sensitive, and frankly you're not gaining any points here. So, if you'll please, excuse me. It's been a long day, and—

ROBERT. —Okay. Just answer this for me then… Please…

(He holds up the form.)

What are my chances with this thing? Really... I don't want to waste my time.

(She considers it for a moment, then gestures for him to take a seat.)

ROSEMARY. All right, Mr. Kahn. Honestly? Not great. Not great because you're single. Not great because you're male. And not great because... Look, the fact that you're...not in a relationship, as I said...not married...not legally permitted to marry is, well...significant.

ROBERT. I see... And the fact that I'm...

ROSEMARY. It's extremely difficult to nurture a child, Mr. Kahn. We seek a traditional family unit, here at Great Lakes. Only the most responsible, stable, emotionally capable adults are chosen.

ROBERT. And I would be considered emotionally unstable?

ROSEMARY. Look, I don't know what it is, Mr. Kahn. Genetics? Socialization? Choice? I have no idea. And I'm not going to debate that with you right now...because my hands are tied. Listen, I'm not... I saw "The Birdcage." I loved it. But at this agency... I'm sorry, but that's just the way it is. Now, I could refer you to another agency, if you'd like.

(She rifles through her Rolodex.)

A friend of mine works at an agency that specializes in babies with crack addiction and fetal alcohol syndrome. They handle babies infected with HIV as well. She's a lovely woman and would be, I'm sure, more than helpful. I also know of an international agency. There are lots of infants from Eastern Europe... Bosnia...Russia. Of course, you'll have to be prepared for medical expenses. It's an industrial wasteland over there, and unfortunately it's caused a lot of health problems.

ROBERT. I see... Well, I'm a teacher. I don't make a lot of... Health problems, huh? I know this sounds terrible, Mrs. Melon, but I don't know that I want a baby with health problems. I know that sounds awful, but why do I have to be the one to take that on?

ROSEMARY. Maybe you should go through a lawyer then. Try for a private adoption. Again, it's a lot more costly, but—

(ROBERT stands, defeated, angry.)

ROBERT. Listen, thanks. You've been very helpful, but I don't think I'll be needing this.

(He hands back the questionnaire and starts off.)

I'm glad you liked "The Birdcage."

(ROSEMARY stands.)

ROSEMARY. Things are changing, Mr. Kahn.

(He turns on her.)

ROBERT. Not fast enough. I feel like I'm running out of time. I'm 37, for Christ sake! By the time you and the rest of the world catch up, it'll be too late. I'll be like eighty. I'm ready now!

(He stands there, seething for a minute.)

You know, I wasn't entirely honest with you before. I never wanted to have children. Peter did. My partner. I just didn't think I could handle it. I didn't feel…qualified. He was so adamant, so sure, and I… Well, I guess I just felt like a child should have a father and a mother. We argued about it for years. In fact, we almost split up over it. Towards the end, when he couldn't walk anymore, I was literally carrying him from room to room. Feeding him. Changing his diapers. He was dying in the most undignified, horrible way, but I was there to help him through. Without questioning whether I was capable or not. I just did it. I had to. So, yes, I do know what it's like…how difficult it is to nurture, Mrs. Melon. To love. I helped someone out of this world. Now, I just want to help bring someone into it. You must understand that. You have a daughter. You must know what it's like to want to—

ROSEMARY. —A son.

ROBERT. Pardon me?

(She clutches her glass of water, unable to look at him.)

ROSEMARY. It was my son that I was on the phone with.

ROBERT. Your son?

ROSEMARY. You assumed it was my daughter, and I didn't correct you.

ROBERT. Oh.

ROSEMARY. It was my son.

ROBERT. I see.

ROSEMARY. He wants a doll… He already has one… But this one does all sorts of things… Pees and poops and cries, and God know what else… His father…

(She finally looks at him.)

That's not a bad thing, is it?

ROBERT. I don't think so.

ROSEMARY. It doesn't necessarily mean…

(She realizes, suddenly, who she's talking to. He sees that she gets it.)

ROBERT. Nope.

(They stand there for a moment, in silence.)

ROBERT. Well…

(At an impasse, ROBERT *slowly starts off again.)*

ROSEMARY. What was the name of the toy store?

ROBERT. Excuse me?

ROSEMARY. Where you found the Baby Cuddles.

ROBERT. Oh… The Toys-R-Us on Vernon.

(He slowly crosses back to her desk.)

What was the name of your friend? At the other agency?

(She smiles and hands him her friend's number.)

Thanks.

(He starts to exit.)

ROSEMARY. Hey, Robert!

(She holds the questionnaire out for him, encouragingly. He looks at it for a moment, then takes it, a slight look of hopefulness on his face as he exits.)

*(*ROSEMARY *watches him go. She sits in silence for a moment, then goes to take a sip of water.)*

(Catching a glimpse at her sad, half-dead plant, she stops for a moment, then pours the water into the pot instead, picking a few of the brown leaves off as the lights fade to black.)

End of Play

Camillia Sanes and Gareth Williams in *187*
Naked Angels at Theater 3 in New York City (1996).

187

by Jose Rivera

BIOGRAPHY

Jose Rivera is the Obie Award winning author of *Marisol, Cloud Tectonics, References to Salvador Dali Make Me Hot,* and *Boleros for the Disenchanted,* among many others. His screenplay for *The Motorcycle Diaries* received an Academy Award nomination for Best Adapted Screenplay.

ACKNOWLEDGMENTS

187 was first produced by Naked Angels at Theater 3 in New York City as a part of *Naked and Hate Free* (July–August, 1996). It was directed by Charlie Stratton with the following cast:

JOHN..Gareth Williams
ALEJANDRA..Camillia Sanes

And the following production staff:

Producer..Geoffrey Nauffts
Set Design..George Xenos
Lighting Design ....Shawn P. Gallagher, James Vermeulen
Sound Design..Rob Gould

CAST OF CHARACTERS

JOHN
ALEJANDRA

187

The City of Industry. Present day. Five P.M.

A bus stop.

ALEJANDRA *waits for a bus. She's exhausted after working an eight hour day in a factory.* JOHN *comes running up to her. He's run a long distance. He's exhausted from working the same job.*

JOHN. *(Out of breath:)* There's something I have to tell you...hi...hi... I'm sorry, hi...

ALEJANDRA. I'm sorry; I'm waiting—

JOHN. *(Catching his breath:)* I—I don't chase people. I have my pride, you know.

ALEJANDRA. I'm waiting for the number eighteen...

JOHN. Pride is very important these days. Not much of it left. 'Specially when you're working a shit job like we are, huh?

ALEJANDRA. ...I think I see it coming. *Ay, gracias a Dios!*

JOHN. The conditions in that place...like a slave labor camp...some gulag... I don't think they're going to pass a hike in the minimum wage... looks like we're stuck in this Dickensian hell...

(The bus passes by. It's not the one ALEJANDRA *is waiting for.)*

ALEJANDRA. No...*carajo*...it's the number six...

JOHN. Dust, cat shit, bad lighting, noise, filth, low pay: it's immoral is what it is; but it's *work,* I guess, and I don't let the work get me down. I have my pride, as I said. I do. That's why I feel odd now, you see? Chasing you. I don't chase people. I don't.

*(*ALEJANDRA *looks at* JOHN *for the first time.)*

ALEJANDRA. You have your pride.

JOHN. *Exactly!* Yes! How did you know?

ALEJANDRA. I do too. I'm waiting for...

JOHN. The number eighteen.

ALEJANDRA. It's late! *Que jodienda! Que mierda!*

JOHN. Hard to have a lotta pride when you're waiting for a bus, I imagine. I've got an old T-bird. Twenty trillion miles. But it's a shit kicker. Red interior. Original everything—except the engine. Which I rebuilt myself. You've probably seen it in the lot. It's right over...

ALEJANDRA. *(Turning to him:)* I don't want to talk to you.

JOHN. ...there. I could drive you... I mean, I swallowed my pride and

159

ran all the way out here chasing you to ask if I could drive you home in my ancient but very cool T-bird. Wanna?

ALEJANDRA. No thank you. It's not personal, *pero no quiero ir contigo. Entiendes?* You see?

JOHN. Not really. I'm John.

ALEJANDRA. *(To herself:) Ay Dios! Si este pendejo no me deja tranquila, me voy a poner a gritar!*

JOHN. You're from a Spanish speaking country. But you don't look like a lot of the Spanish speakers at the plant. You are, uh…well…they're kinda smaller…they have more Indian, I guess, features…dark…and eyes that really penetrate…you don't know what their minds are doing…you look into their eyes and it's like looking into an infinite tunnel that goes into this deep ancient place and all you can see is this dark alphabet that's spelling words and feelings that you can't read. You're not like them. *Your* eyes aren't so…unfathomable. There's light in that tunnel. A sparkle. Something I can recognize and read. A friendliness. Like you don't wanna, you know, cut me up on some Mayan pyramid and offer my heart to some jealous horrible god. You're not gonna do that! There's a frightening, primitive *distance* I feel with the other Spanish speakers at work. But you're different. You're a different branch of the Spanish speaking world. Where is your home? Where?

ALEJANDRA. Argentina.

JOHN. *(Smiles.)* That makes sense. There's something more Italian about you than those Guatemalan chicks I see all the time. A Sophia Loren kinda quality…

ALEJANDRA. What do you want? I don't want to ride in your car! Can't you tell that? I don't want to talk to you. How much more silent do I have to be to get you to go away? Do I have to slap your face? I'm not afraid of you. Some of the girls at work, maybe, are afraid of to say something when they're harassed, but I am not. Is that what you want from me?

JOHN. Whoa, back up…

ALEJANDRA. You have no idea who I am. I am not Sophia Loren!

JOHN. I *know*…

ALEJANDRA. My family is political. My family has died in Argentina for political reasons. Do you know what I had to do to get here? Do you think there is anything you can do to frighten me? *Puerco! Cabron!*

JOHN. Just want to say hello. I don't know. You don't have to…

ALEJANDRA. I get up at five o'clock. I take two buses to get here, I work my…*como se dice*…my ass off for *no money*…and I take two buses to get home and you want to talk about my *sparkle?!*

JOHN. It's irresistible.

ALEJANDRA. *Idiota!*

JOHN. That didn't sound like a compliment!

ALEJANDRA. *Hijo de la puta madre!*

JOHN. I know what *that* is!

ALEJANDRA. Only a man could see through the sweat and filth in that building, the chemical smell, and the smell of rat poison, the dim lighting and monotony and cold and think of *sex*.

JOHN. A powerful drug.

ALEJANDRA. You don't know. North Americans don't know. There's an art to it. A culture of love. It needs the right conditions in order to live…

JOHN. I think it's got the right conditions right now.

ALEJANDRA. And I don't mean it can't be difficult. I know of people in prison who fall in love. People on their death beds. People without any other hope. And love finds its way to them and transforms them. I don't mean it has to be *easy;* but it does have to be *right*…

JOHN. Who's talking about love anyway? I just wanna drive you home in my car. I don't want you to wear yourself out taking four buses every day. I don't want to see you breaking your back any more than you have to. I'm offering you something good in your completely shitty day. I didn't imply anything else. You—*you*—brought up sex and love, not me!

ALEJANDRA. Then…excuse me. My mistake.

JOHN. I have feelings too. Latin Americans don't corner the market on feelings!

ALEJANDRA. But I did already say no to the ride and that's all I have to say about it.

(Short beat.)

JOHN. Yeah, that's fine. You can do that. You say no it's no. I'm not from the 1950s when no didn't mean jackshit to a man. I know what *"pendejo"* means: you can't call me that 'cause I ain't one! I was drawn to the light reflected in your eyes. It warms me. I don't get enough of that light in my life. Thought if you spent a little time in my car as I drove you home you could tell me about your world and I'd be able to enjoy that light a few extra minutes. Because I live in darkness. I live in a pit. I live among the moles and shrews and earthworms, all these eyeless creatures digging in the shit of the world looking for their love and their sex. You're the one person I've seen in a year in this city that's got more than survival on their minds, whose laughter I've heard louder and clearer than all the sounds of all the machinery in that fucking plant. I thought I could live on that a few extra minutes a day. To keep me from suffocating in the darkness. You have *that much* you could hold over me. That much. And I don't have anything. No money, no degrees, no family, no politics: just a pathetic old car my older brother gave me 'cause he felt sorry for me.

(*Beat.*)

The only thing I have, I guess, is that I live here. I'm American. And you're not. I have this country and its laws. And you don't. You have your papers, honey? You have that green card? You have a right to be standing here waiting for my bus? Using up my roads and my housing? I've seen it happen before—I've seen the company call Immigration every time there's a little agitation at the plant. Union talk. Unhappy workers. I've seen it. It's not nice. The place goes crazy when those agents appear. You see old people running pretty fast! I'd laugh—I would—I'd laugh watching those pretty legs running from the INS like a dog!

(*Beat.*)

I'm sorry. Forget that. Sounding like a fucking Nazi asshole. I don't mean to make threats to you. I'm not the kind to do that. I guess it's the only power I thought I had over you. And I guess I don't even have that.

ALEJANDRA. I didn't live through the worst of it: I was too young. But I heard stories from my family. Stories always told in whispers. My uncle lived in Buenos Aires. He said during the worst of it he and my aunt would hear two or three explosions a night. The left bombing the right, the right bombing the left. And he said he got to the point where he knew, by the sound the explosion made, whether or not there had been a human being in that explosion. We had a neighbor. Old man. A doctor. He used to work with the military making sure the torture didn't kill the prisoners. As a doctor he knew how to keep political prisoners alive so the army could rape and torture more and more. The power those men had in those rooms was absolute. They are gone—but they are not really gone.

(*Beat. She looks at him.*)

Hey John: go ahead. Send me back.

(*The two wait together. Blackout.*)

End of Play

Richard Bekins, Lou Liberatore, and Dan Goldman in *Love*
Naked Angels at Theater 3 in New York City (1996).

LOVE
by Daniel Reitz

BIOGRAPHY

Daniel Reitz is a playwright and screenwriter living in New York City. His plays have been developed and produced at theatres including the Mark Taper Forum, Manhattan Class Company, Ensemble Studio Theatre, Naked Angels, New York Stage and Film, Playwrights Horizons, and the Joseph Papp Public Theatre, and in London at the White Bear and Oval House theatres. He adapted his play *Urban Folk Tales* as the feature film *Urbania*, which premiered at the Sundance Film Festival, and won "Best Film" prizes in Los Angeles, Philadelphia, Provincetown, and San Francisco film festivals prior to being released by Lions Gate Films. He has also written and directed several short films, which have screened at film festivals in the United States, Europe, Australia and Asia. He has received a New York Innovative Theatre Award, a Drama-Logue Award and a New York Foundation for the Arts fiction fellowship, a playwriting commission from the Lower Manhattan Cultural Council, and artist residencies from the Edward Albee Foundation, the Hawthornden Castle International Retreat for Writers in Scotland, the MacDowell Colony, the Virginia Center for the Creative Arts, and the Yaddo Corporation. His plays have been published by Smith and Kraus, Plays and Playwrights 2008 (New York Theatre Experience), and United Stages. He is a member of New Dramatists.

ACKNOWLEDGMENTS

Love was first produced by Naked Angels at Theater 3 in New York City as a part of *Naked and Hate Free* (July–August, 1996). It was directed by Charlie Stratton with the following cast:

JERRY .... Richard Bekins
GARY .... Lou Liberatore
MARK .... Dan Goldman

And the following production staff:

Producer .... Geoffrey Nauffts
Set Design .... George Xenos
Lighting Design .... Shawn P. Gallagher,
James Vermeulen
Sound Design .... Rob Gould

CAST OF CHARACTERS

JERRY, 40s
GARY, 40s
MARK, 20s

TIME AND PLACE

New York. Spring. Evening.

LOVE

The living room of a New York apartment.

GARY *sits in a leather club chair.* JERRY *sits in another leather club chair, opposite him.* MARK *stands between them.* JERRY *and* MARK *are drinking whiskey from tumblers. There is the sound of a porn video emanating from a TV, nearby.*

JERRY. So.

MARK. So.

JERRY. *(Drinks.)* Mmmmnn. *(Holds glass.)* Whaddya think?

MARK. Pretty good.

JERRY. Twenty-five year-old Laphroaig, a hundred-fifty bucks a bottle, yeah I'd say pretty good.

MARK. *(Swishes whiskey around in glass.)* Pretty good if you like peat moss.

*(*JERRY *laughs.)*

This shit's older than I am.

JERRY. Oh, to be younger than a bottle of booze. Bet you don't get much cause to drink hundred-fifty-buck scotch, do ya?

*(*JERRY *smiles, pouring his glass of whiskey on the floor. Silence.)*

MARK. Actually my dad's a scotch drinker.

JERRY. Is he? *(Laughs.)* Dad.

MARK. What.

JERRY. Dad. The word. Outta your mouth. Makes me wanna hafta chortle like.

MARK. Why's that.

JERRY. I thought your kind didn't have "dads." I mean, what I picture when you say the word "dad" is a fat Schlitz-swilling pederast indoctrinating you with repeated prepubescent ass pluggings into your present state of amorality and decay. Is what I mean.

*(*JERRY *and* MARK *look at one another.)*

MARK. He's a lawyer. Dad. Tax attorney.

JERRY. Make a good living, does he?

MARK. Pretty good, yeah.

(Pause.)

JERRY. Yeah, get your shirt off.

*(*MARK *smiles at* JERRY, *then slowly downs his glass of whiskey. He peels his T-shirt off and tosses it onto the floor.)*

169

(Tenderly, smiling:) C'mere.

> (MARK *walks over to where* JERRY *sits.* JERRY *unzips Mark's pants and reaches in to feel* MARK *as he speaks.*)

This is what you have to do to get by, huh? This is what you're reduced to? So sad. What kind of father is it who reduces his son to this?

> (MARK *laughs.*)

He sucked your little dick, didn't he? You can tell me, Mark. Don't hold back.

MARK. *(Smiles.)* OK. I won't.

JERRY. He fingered your little adolescent butthole, didn't he?

MARK. Mmmmmnnnn.

> (MARK *looks over at* GARY, *who sits and watches them.*)

You all right over there?

JERRY. He's fine, he's fine, he just, he forgets he's alive sometimes. An honest mistake.

MARK. *(To* JERRY:*)* So, uh…he just gonna watch? 'Cause, uh…I got a strict ya know, rule…even if you're just gonna watch it's still gonna cost. If there are two physical humans in the room…

> (JERRY *withdraws his hand from Mark's pants. Pause.*)

JERRY. One seventy-five, right?

MARK. Each. *(To* GARY:*)* What's your name, again?

GARY. Gary.

MARK. Hey, Gary. *(To* JERRY:*)* And you're Jerry. That's funny.

JERRY. It is, isn't it? We're a joke, all right, like a Christ-fucking sitcom taped live from Hades.

> *(Pause.)*

It's his birthday. And your dick is my gift to him. And don't worry about your goddamn money. Three hundred-fifty an hour, what would that be a minute?

MARK. Five eighty-three.

JERRY. *(Smiles, admiringly.)* Five dollars and eighty-three cents a minute. You got it right down to the three cents. I love that. You little bitch. *(Laughs.)* Still. Doesn't seem like all that much. When you break down minutes into seconds, when every second is a single thrust inside some moist undesired begging sphincter. What's the easiest hundred seventy-five you ever made, Mark?

MARK. Ah…that would have to be last summer, this old guy into obscene spandex display in public paid me to dress up in these really tight shorts with nothin' on underneath and walk around outside with him for an hour. I mean, these things would've fit a four-year-old. Jaws were fallin'. *(Shrugs.)* All he wanted.

JERRY. You do much of this thing, this three-way shit?

MARK. Yes and no.

JERRY. What the fuck does that mean?

MARK. *(To* GARY:*)* How long you two been together?

JERRY. Where do you get off talking to *him?* Talk to *me.* I'm the one who's paying ya. Christ.

　　(Pause.)

GARY. Twelve years. We've been together twelve years. Twelve years today we first met. At the old Thalia Ninety-fifth Street. In the rain.

　　(Pause.)

JERRY. So. The nonentity reminisces.

MARK. Awww. In the rain even. So. *(Smiles.)* Is this kinda thing the secret behind your longevity, then?

JERRY. Secret? There's no fucking secret. I'll tell ya what it is: it's a gnawing on the abscess of denial for twelve years.

MARK. Huh. Great.

JERRY. Until the irrevocable realization: that he who swears he's always loved you has, in fact, lied. That he has been with you out of habit, out of fear, out of some shopworn weary affection…but not love. And not want. And when all you've got *is* that…*want*…the want that eats your balls away… And the longing…

But you do without. You get up every day and every day you do without, Chinese take-out, a movie, a show, SoHo, Bucks County weekends. And you tell yourself that you can live like this, because at the very least there he is beside you every night.

Until the fateful day the stranger enters into the picture.

(To GARY:*)* We all know about the stranger, don't we, dear? Oh yes. And the inevitable desertion? Preceding the tedious betrayal?

(To MARK:*)* This is our mutual punishment. He's going to get fucked in front of me and I'm going to watch. Now you're going to fuck him and I want you to make sure it hurts.

　　(Pause.)

MARK. I could use another drink.

JERRY. Tough. Get to work.

> *(MARK stares at JERRY.)*

MARK. This isn't all I do, ya know.

JERRY. Is that right? So what else are ya, literacy volunteer?

GARY. He's a student.

> *(Pause.)*

MARK. *(To GARY:)* Yeah. That's right. Good guess. *(To JERRY:)* I'm a student.

JERRY. *(Laughs.)* Perfect! Don't even tell me. Law. Just like Dad.

MARK. Maybe. Eventually.

JERRY. Oh Jee-zuz. Make me puke.

> *(MARK smiles, walks over to where GARY sits. He pulls GARY up from his chair by his belt.)*

MARK. So…this is what you want, birthday boy?

> *(MARK kisses GARY, a long sensual kiss on the mouth. He places GARY's hands on his bare chest.)*

JERRY. No tenderness, ya got that? I'm not shellin' out for any goddamn face-sucking.

MARK. You want me to fuck you, huh? 'Cause I *want* to…

> *(MARK turns, smiles at JERRY, then kisses GARY again, another deep, sensual kiss. He licks GARY's neck. GARY closes his eyes.)*

GARY. And what's your girlfriend's name?

> *(Pause. MARK stops, hearing this. Then, he slowly starts to unbutton Gary's shirt.)*

MARK. Zoë.

JERRY. Yeah, right, *girlfriend.* Like we won't see your ass in the Lure two nights from now.

GARY. Do you love her?

MARK. She's great. Oh, I so wanna *fuck* you, man…

JERRY. Look: I don't want any unnecessary fraternizing between you two faggots.

GARY. Does she mind what you do?

JERRY. Just. Get. To it.

> *(Pause.)*

MARK. We don't talk about it.

GARY. She doesn't know.

MARK. Not really.

GARY. She'd be upset.

MARK. Yeah.

JERRY. I am *waiting* here.

GARY. But you love her?

> *(Pause.)*

MARK. Uh... *(Laughs.)* Well. I want to be with her. For now, anyway. Are you sure you're...uh...

> *(GARY takes MARK's hands in his own.)*

GARY. Let me tell you about love. What I know. Our last night together, when I knew I'd never see him again...

JERRY. Shut the fuck up.

GARY. I told him, I said, the problem is you're obsessed—

JERRY. You do not speak. You hear me?

> *(Pause. JERRY and GARY stare at each other. GARY looks back to MARK.)*

GARY. Problem is you're obsessed, and he agreed without looking at me.

JERRY. You do not mention 'he,' you hear me? 'He' has no place in these proceedings. You get fucked. Only. With your mouth shut.

GARY. No, that isn't how it works. This is how it works: I speak now, you listen. *Mutual* punishment. Remember? And if you interrupt me again I'll take my birthday present into the bedroom and lock the door. And we don't want that, do we? Dear?

> *(Silence, as they look at each other. Then, GARY looks back to MARK.)*

I was thinking how we'd met a few months before, my stranger and I...this time no rain...no movie theater...no romance...just this dark dive bar... and how he'd looked at me, like he wanted me or wanted me dead. We went back to his place and I took up residence in his bed for a week. He wouldn't let me sleep, or brush my teeth or even eat. It was as if I existed for one reason only.

For him.

> *(JERRY laughs. GARY looks at him. Silence.)*

And it went on like this. And on. And I was delirious. My old life...*this*... all over. Done with. *(To JERRY:)* I was never coming back. *(To MARK:)* I thought. And I was high...elated...

But now, that night, there were tears in his eyes. Because things had changed. Because he'd met someone else.

JERRY. Awww.

GARY. How amazing to see this fifty-two-year-old ex-bartender, ex-welder, ex-mineworker, present union crewman, this force of nature, a Welshman—he was Welsh—so *reduced* by a skinny twenty-three-year-old *Beauty and the Beast* chorus boy. But there it was. The man loved Broadway. *(Laughs.)* It all started one rainy matinee day when my Welshman was moving scenery backstage. And there was the chorus boy. And what began as a little flirtation became full-blown obsession for my Welshman. To which this twenty-three year-old chorus boy responded, with the petulance of the entitled. And from there on it was the chorus boy and only the chorus boy for him. He was captive. We both knew this would be our last time together. He was sorry but he didn't see any way. It was getting impossible. The chorus boy was a prickly number. Tyrannical. Had to be appeased. Handled with kid gloves. See, the problem was...*the chorus boy was in love with him.* That's what he said to me, tears in his eyes. A sad delusion on the part of my Welshman, but there it was. It didn't matter if I pointed out his delusion, he never would have believed it. The problem was, chorus boy yea or chorus boy nay, my love loved *him.* And I'm not a scene-maker. Besides which I didn't want our last time to be some pointless argument.

But I said will you do something. I was caressing his hand...

    (GARY caresses MARK's hand.)

...stroking his fingers. Beautiful large hands I so loved. And he said what is it. And I told him, and before he could say anything I kissed him...

JERRY. *(Suddenly pained:)* Don't.

    (GARY kisses MARK.)

GARY. ...and rolled over onto my stomach. I didn't say anything, I just waited. And he was quiet for a long time, and then I heard him get up, I heard him rustling around, and then he came back. I could hear him doing something with his hands, a slick sound, and without even seeing them I thought again of those hands rough and callused from years of...Welsh labor, and I breathed slowly as he slid in one, then two, then three, four fingers...

    (JERRY closes his eyes.)

Then the thumb...and I could feel myself tighten when the bone of his wrist made it inside...I was afraid he's stop but he wouldn't, he kept reaching inside and the pain was...it was...*incredible...excruciating*...but then it receded...and as he reached in and reached in...we breathed together, deep inhale, deep exhale, deeply, deeply...

    (JERRY opens his eyes. His glass drops from his hand. It rolls on the carpet, whiskey spilling.)

Later he'd told me he'd felt my heart beating…pulsing…the vibrations coursing through him. But I've since wondered if he was telling me the truth. You say all sorts of things when you love someone. And when you don't…

(GARY *looks at* JERRY.)

You don't say anything. Nothing at all.

(*Silence.* JERRY *and* GARY *stare at each other.*)

(*The sound of the porn video from the TV fills the silence.*)

(*Lights fade.*)

End of Play

May 30, 1997

Warm greetings to everyone gathered in Los Angeles for the performance of "GunPlay."

Gun violence, in one way or another, has touched every community in America, and it has taken an especially devastating toll on our young people. By using the power of drama to focus on this crucial issue, "GunPlay" challenges audiences to recognize the need to confront gun violence and to devise effective solutions. This is an example of how the arts can help us creatively address the problems facing our nation today.

My Administration is working hard to make America safer, fighting for strict gun control laws and putting more law enforcement officers on the streets. But government alone cannot end the violence that plagues too many of our communities. I applaud you for your efforts to raise awareness of this difficult problem and its costs and consequences to our society. Working together, we can ensure a safer, brighter future for us all.

Best wishes for a memorable evening.

Bill Clinton

gunplay

LA FAMILIA
by Seth Zvi Rosenfeld

BIOGRAPHY

Seth Zvi Rosenfeld was born and raised in NYC. His newest play *Handball* will be produced in New York next season. His most recent play, *Everything's Turning Into Beautiful,* opened July, 2006 at The New Group. It starred Daphne Rubin-Vega and Malik Yoba.

Mr. Rosenfeld is currently developing *Snitch,* a TV series for A&E, with Warner Horizon and John Wells Productions. He is currently writing the book for a Broadway musical version of the movie *Superfly,* with Tommy Mottola and Jeb Brien producing. He most recently worked with Tommy Mottola and Antoine Fuqua to create an hour series based on the book *Queens Reigns Supreme* for Showtime. He also developed a series for FX titled *Cop and His Son* with Sony TV and Tantemount producing. He developed a series for CBS titled *On Behalf Of The Dead.* He wrote and executive produced *Wyclef Jean In America* for HBO with Wyclef Jean, Mary J. Blige, Robert Klein, and Danny Hoch.

Only In New York, a movie script that he wrote with Geebee Dejani is being developed by Tucker Tooley and Dan Keston. The movie will star Jim Caviezel, Ray Liotta, and Gerard Depardu and will be directed by Pitof. Mr. Rosenfeld will direct his original screenplay, *Lessons For Benny Blanco,* with Amy Robinson producing, and it will star Victor Rasuk and Zoe Saldana. His screenplay *Suicide Drills* is being packaged by CAA for Al Pacino to star. He is an Adjunct Professor in the graduate film studies at Columbia University.

As a filmmaker, Mr. Rosenfeld has written and directed the feature films, *A Brother's Kiss* (First Look/Overseas) and *King of the Jungle* (Sony/Urbanworld). His films have appeared in many national and international festivals including Venice and Deauville. He was invited to participate in the Sundance Institutes Writers and Directors labs. His award winning short *Under the Bridge* ran for several years on BRAVO.

He wrote and directed a segment of *Subway Stories* for HBO, which Geebee Dajani co-wrote, and he directed *We Deliver* for Palm Pictures. He wrote the feature film, *Sunset Park,* for Jersey films/Tri-Star and has worked extensively as a writer and script doctor in film and television for New Line Cinema, Universal Pictures, Tri-star Pictures, Polygram, Gramercy, Island Pictures, Columbia Pictures, Twentieth Century Fox, Warner TV, HBO, and UPN.

Mr. Rosenfeld started his career as a playwright nurtured by the Ensemble Studio Theatre and the now defunct Double Image and Angel Theatre companies. His plays include *The Writing on the Wall,* produced by the Westbeth Theatre Center; *The Blackeyed Brothers,* produced by Double Image Theatre and winner of the Samuel French short play award; *A Brother's Kiss* and *After the Marching Stopped,* produced by Angel Theatre at Intar and re-titled *Brothers. Mothers and Others; Servy-n-Bernice 4ever,* directed by Terry Kinney and produced commercially Off-Broadway at the Provincetown Playhouse; *A Passover Story,* commissioned by the late Joseph Papp for the Public Theatre; *The Flatted Fifth,* produced by The New Group; the tiny plays *La Familia, My Starship,* and *P.S: I'm glad you sent your hair* for Naked Angels and the Hip-Hop Theatre festival. Many of his plays have been published by Samuel French. He is a member of the New York Playwright's Lab.

ACKNOWLEDGMENTS

La Familia was first produced by Naked Angels at The Actors Gang in Los Angeles as a part of *Gunplay* (May 23–June 15, 1997). It was directed by Paul S. Eckstein with the following:

MINGITA .... Tracy Vilar
RALPHIE .... Doug Spain

And the following production staff:

Producers .... Veronica Brady,
                                                     Paul S. Eckstein, Tim Ransom
Co-Producer .... Toni Kotite
Associate Producers .... Laura Salvato, Mark Seldis
Set Designer .... Stephanie Kerley Schwartz
Costume Designer .... Dana Allyson
Lighting Designer .... David Hahn

CAST OF CHARACTERS

MINGITA
RALPHIE

TIME AND PLACE

Irey-Irey Jamaican Health Food Store. Now.

LA FAMILIA

MINGITA, *17, and butch as they come, sits in the back of the store bagging up weed with* RALPHIE, *18.*

MINGITA. Know what this nigga said?

RALPHIE. What he said?

MINGITA. He said, he'd make one phone call and somebody was gonna come shoot us.

RALPHIE. One phone call? …Did you short him on that bag?

MINGITA. I'm sayin' the kid was like twelve years old.

RALPHIE. He was fourteen.

MINGITA. That kid was twelve.

RALPHIE. He's fourteen.

MINGITA. Twelve.

RALPHIE. Fourteen.

MINGITA. Whatever… My point is why do niggas always say that shit?

RALPHIE. What?

MINGITA. I'll make one phone call and blah, blah, blah…

RALPHIE. Check it, I was uptown to pick up a package for Chinito, right. I had like three grand in my pocket but I'm too cheap to take a cab, right.

MINGITA. Why are you so stupid, Ralphie?

RALPHIE. Anyway, I'm on the two train uptown and these niggas rolled in, like fifty deep, I'm talkin' 'bout Bronx cavemen, fifty deep up in this two train.

MINGITA. True.

RALPHIE. So they start wildin', right… They pull off this ladies chain, punch this old man in his mouth and I'm sittin' there holdin' my dick with three grand in my pocket and nowhere to go. Yeah.

So like seven of them surround me and asked me for my gold and all I'm thinkin' is Chinito is gonna murder me for not takin' a cab, right.

MINGITA. So what happened?

RALPHIE. I told them I ain't givin' up shit… This kid slapped me like I was a bitch, I got heated and swung and missed, when I had like fifty guns pointed at me…

MINGITA. Coño— Ralphie, what did you do?

RALPHIE. I said lemme tell you something, my name is Ralphie Camacho, I'm a straight Latin King from the lower east, I ain't givin' y'all shit, y'all better fuckin' kill me cause I'll make one phone call and there'll be bodies all over the

MINGITA. So what'd they do?

RALPHIE. They fronted... They said this kid is crazy, leave him alone.

MINGITA. Get the fuck outta here.

RALPHIE. Word to mother, Mingita, that shit worked.

MINGITA. Yeah but you still ain't answer the question.

RALPHIE. What's that?

MINGITA. Who was you gonna call with that one phone call?

RALPHIE. Oh, I don't know... Probably you.

> *(They both laugh.)*

RALPHIE. Who would you call?

MINGITA. Yo, light up that Chronic, Ralphie.

RALPHIE. I ain't stealin' from Chinito.

MINGITA. Take a little fuckin' pinch out of each bag and we'll smoke it.

RALPHIE. I ain't stealin' from Chinito.

MINGITA. I'm not tryin' to steal from fuckin' Chinito... Even if he is a fuckin' cheap bastard. I'm sayin' just tap each bag a tiny-tiny bit.

RALPHIE. So you did short that kid on that bag.

MINGITA. I can't believe you said that...

RALPHIE. You just told me to tap the bags so we could get high.

MINGITA. Let me tell you something. I have never stolen from nobody in my fuckin' life! ...Okay.

RALPHIE. Yeah well Chinito asked me yesterday if I had been tappin' the bags... He said somebody's been doin' it.

MINGITA. So it has to be me then, right?

RALPHIE. We the only ones workin', right?

MINGITA. Has it ever occurred to you that Chinito might be fuckin' paranoid? That he might be sniffin' too much of that Terminator and that motherfucker is trippin'? Has that ever occurred to you?

RALPHIE. Mingita, that kid who said you shorted him has an older brother named Boo-boo who's a fuckin' gangster.

MINGITA. So?

RALPHIE. What if he comes in here and shoots us?

MINGITA. I'll get my big brother to shoot his big brother.

RALPHIE. You don't have no big brother.

MINGITA. I do so.

RALPHIE. Mingita, I know your whole fuckin' family.

MINGITA. Why they gotta be my "fuckin' family."

RALPHIE. What?

MINGITA. What you just said, why they gotta be my "fuckin' family."

RALPHIE. I'm just sayin' you don't have a big brother.

MINGITA. That's how much you know, I got a big brother in fuckin' Staten Island.

RALPHIE. In Staten Island?

MINGITA. In Staten Island.

RALPHIE. You never been to Staten Island in your life, maybe Riker's Island but not Staten Island.

MINGITA. You don't know where I go after work.

RALPHIE. I see you every day, Mingita.

MINGITA. Fuck you, Ralphie. Don't do that... Don't ever do that.

RALPHIE. Do what?

MINGITA. Cross the line with me... Try to get in my business.

RALPHIE. It ain't no fuckin' big deal, Mingita... I ain't got no big brother and if I did he probably wouldn't give a fuck about me anyway... That's why I live in Helga House... My family don't give a fuck about me.

MINGITA. Yeah well, that's your business... My family is fine.

RALPHIE. Then how come you live in the buildin' with the squatters?

MINGITA. I don't live with no fuckin' squatters.

RALPHIE. I seen you up in there with the fuckin' whiteboy squatters.

MINGITA. I hang out with those motherfuckers, I don't live there.

RALPHIE. That's why all your clothes is up in there.

MINGITA. My girl stays up in there... You don't know where I live. I got places to stay, I could stay uptown, in the Bronx, Brooklyn, Staten Island, Jersey, Miami, Puerto Rico, The Dominican Republic.

RALPHIE. Oh I got it, you just choose to stay with those dirty, roach ass, whiteboy squatters... I got it.

MINGITA. See if I punch you in the mouth I'd be wrong, right?

(MINGITA *swings wildly at* RALPHIE. RALPHIE *blocks it.*)

RALPHIE. I'm your best fuckin' friend! How you gonna hit me? What the fuck is wrong with you?

MINGITA. If you was my best friend, you'd stop frontin' and get me high.

RALPHIE. Fuck you, Mingita, I'm not doin' it.

MINGITA. I'm takin' your shit then.

(MINGITA grabs a bag from RALPHIE.)

RALPHIE. Gimme the fuckin' bag, Mingita.

MINGITA. What you gonna do? Hit me? Tell Chinito, you little fuckin' bitch ass motherfucker… What you gonna do?

RALPHIE. Can I please have the bag?

MINGITA. No… Lemme ask you somethin', you little faggot, why you go and tell that kid I was your sister.

RALPHIE. You and him was arguin', and I was just sayin' leave my sister alone.

MINGITA. I ain't your sister, Ralphie. You're far too ugly to be my brother… I ain't your fuckin' sister.

RALPHIE. Fuck you then, you ain't my sister… Smoke your fuckin' little reefer you ain't nothin' but a weedhead anyway.

MINGITA. See, why I gotta be a weedhead…

RALPHIE. That's all you care about. Stealin' from customers, gettin' us in trouble.

MINGITA. If I light this up you ain't gonna smoke with me?

RALPHIE. Hell no.

MINGITA. You don't love me.

RALPHIE. I fuckin' hate you, Mingita.

MINGITA. Why?

RALPHIE. 'Cause you're a bitch.

MINGITA. How you gonna call me out my name, Ralphie? …How you gonna disrespect me like that?

RALPHIE. You're the one who said I'm too fuckin' ugly to be your brother.

MINGITA. I was playin'.

RALPHIE. Well I wasn't.

MINGITA. You wanna be my brother, for real?

RALPHIE. I did… I used to… Not no more.

MINGITA. Oh really… You care about me that much?

RALPHIE. Not no more…

MINGITA. What would you have done if that kid pulled on me?

RALPHIE. What would I have done? …I'd have taken the bullet for you.

MINGITA. You'd have done that for me?

RALPHIE. No doubt.

MINGITA. You'd have taken the bullet?

RALPHIE. Yup.

MINGITA. ...That's fucked up.

RALPHIE. What?

MINGITA. That's the nicest thing anybody ever said to me...

(MINGITA *tries to stop herself from crying.*)

RALPHIE. You're drama, Mingita.

MINGITA. Will you roll this shit for me? Please you roll better than me... I got these fuckin' nails.

RALPHIE. You know Chinito's gonna kill us if he finds out.

MINGITA. I don't care... I'll take a bullet for you, Ralphie.

RALPHIE. You would?

MINGITA. ...We family, right?

RALPHIE. Right...

MINGITA. Let's get high.

End of Play

fear

THE ONLY OTHER OPTION
by Patrick Breen

BIOGRAPHY

Patrick Breen is a writer and actor. He has been a member of Naked Angels almost from the beginning. An evening of his one act plays, *Saturday Mourning Cartoons* was produced there. His plays have also been performed at MCC and The Atlantic. His play *Marking* was made into a movie titled *Just A Kiss* directed by Fisher Stevens. As an actor Mr. Breen appeared in the film *Ishtar* and the television program *21 Jump Street*.

ACKNOWLEDGMENTS

The Only Other Option was first produced by Naked Angels at Greenwich Street Theater in New York City as a part of *Fear* (February 13–March 2, 2003). It was directed by Lizzie Gottlieb with the following cast:

WOMAN .... Maria Tucci
HEAD .... Timothy Britten Parker

And the following production staff:

Producer .... Sherri Kotimsky
Set Design .... Asaki Oda
Lighting Design .... Peter Hoerburger
Costume Design .... Brad Scoggins
Sound Design .... A. Stanley Gurczak
Original Music .... Rick Baitz

CAST OF CHARACTERS

WOMAN
HEAD

THE ONLY OTHER OPTION

A man's HEAD *appears from out of the darkness, perched atop a metal table covered in a silvery cloth. The* HEAD *opens its eyes and blinks. It is alone. There are two blue tubes and a single red tube attached to the base of its neck.*

A WOMAN *enters. She wears a white lab coat and appears to be some kind of doctor or scientist. Around her waist is a belt which holds what looks to be several tubes of lipstick.*

WOMAN. Good afternoon.

HEAD. Mud effa nun.

(The WOMAN *takes one of the small tubes from her belt, opens it and applies some of the colorless substance to the* HEAD's *lips.)*

WOMAN. There is a short period for facial musculature adjustment.

(The HEAD *rubs his lips together and makes three popping sounds.)*

WOMAN. Better?

HEAD. Yes.

WOMAN. How do you feel?

HEAD. I don't know. Okay I guess.

WOMAN. Good.

HEAD. What? Where?

(The HEAD *tries to look around.)*

Oww!

WOMAN. What do you remember?

(The HEAD *thinks.)*

HEAD. That's odd. I don't remember anything.

WOMAN. I can explain.

HEAD. I'm all ears.

(The WOMAN *smiles but the* HEAD *doesn't get the joke.)*

WOMAN. Early in the 21st century you were cryogenically frozen. Your post mortem body was processed then put into a liquid nitrogen bath suspending cell deterioration.

HEAD. Post mortem?

WOMAN. Yes. After your death.

HEAD. I'm dead?

WOMAN. Were dead. You were involved in an accident. You were 38 years old. Is any of this sounding familiar?

HEAD. Nope.

WOMAN. Prior to death you had presciently allocated a sum of your estate to pay for cryogenic maintenance in perpetuity. Or until such time medicine developed a cure for whatever it was that killed you. Your hope was to return to life.

HEAD. Huh.

WOMAN. And here you are. Your hope realized.

HEAD. In the future?

WOMAN. It is the year 2129.

HEAD. Wow. Earlier, I thought you said, I may have misheard, but didn't you say something about freezing my body?

WOMAN. Did I? Oh. No. You opted for the partial cryogenesis. Obviously.

HEAD. Ah.

WOMAN. Just your head.

HEAD. I have a question.

WOMAN. Naturally.

HEAD. *(With rising panic:)* I imagine my predecapitation hope was that if medicine had advanced significantly enough to revive my head, they could, and I'm just guessing here, they could, figure out a way to stick a fucking body under it!

WOMAN. Try to remain calm.

HEAD. Lady, I'm not staying fucking calm! I'm a fucking head!

(The WOMAN *puts the* HEAD *in a headlock.)*

HEAD. Cut that out!

(The WOMAN *applies another tube of lip stuff to the* HEAD's *lips. The* HEAD *calms. He pops his lips three time.)*

HEAD. That stuff is amazing.

(The WOMAN *applies something to her own lips.)*

WOMAN. Mnnnnhmmmm.

HEAD. What are you using?

WOMAN. This is just some color.

HEAD. Suits you.

(The WOMAN *is flattered.)*

WOMAN. Thank you.

HEAD. You're welcome.

WOMAN. The company responsible for your perpetual care declared bankruptcy half a century ago. The government generously agreed to maintain the costly operations until a solution could be worked out. Eventually a decision was made to save only a portion of the nearly 22,000 tanks. Yours was one of the fortunate few.

HEAD. I see.

WOMAN. We have revived you and you are here to experience a second life.

HEAD. I have cheated death.

WOMAN. It would seem so.

HEAD. Remarkable. Will my memory return?

WOMAN. Artifacts, wisps, mostly though we have been unsuccessful.

HEAD. Okay. Well whoever I was, I didn't want to die. And I haven't. I suppose I sort of owe it to the guy to try and live as fully as possible.

WOMAN. That's a wonderful attitude.

HEAD. Plenty of people probably have it worse. I can't think of any at the moment but who cares about that? Suppose I am the worst off person in the world. I'm alive. It's not perfect but what is? And all those skeptics who thought this was impossible, where are they? Huh? And who knows, maybe in a few years science will advance even further and I'll get a torso and some robotic limbs and pretty soon I'll be grabbing a beer and traveling to distant planets and everything imaginable. Okay. This is better than okay. I'm happy.

WOMAN. There is one more thing.

HEAD. Yes.

WOMAN. At considerable cost the government has maintained your care and financed the research that led to your reanimation. They would now like something in return.

HEAD. Understandable. What would they like?

WOMAN. They would like you to wrestle.

HEAD. Beg pardon?

WOMAN. You are familiar with wrestling?

HEAD. I think so.

WOMAN. The rules have remained rather consistent since your time. You won't be in the ring alone. You will have a full-bodied partner. Your life support, those blue tubes attached at your base, will be elastic and strong. You will be flung at your opponent, another wrestler with a head partner, who will, simultaneously be flung at you. You will wear a helmet. If you should prove popular, you will win.

HEAD. They want me to wrestle.

WOMAN. Well, to be accurate, your partner will be wrestling, you will be more of a projectile.

HEAD. *(Panic:)* Lips, lips, lips.

        (The WOMAN *rushes to the* HEAD, *quickly applying lip stuff.)*

HEAD. I absolutely refuse!

WOMAN. Then you will wrestle against your will and you will lose. I urge you to reconsider. Wrestlers are interplanetary celebrities. They are royalty. Their lives are front screen news. To place this in historical perspective, the hysteria surrounding each bout falls somewhere between World Cup and World War.

HEAD. You know what? This is obviously not the future I had in mind. No harm, no foul. Refreeze me.

WOMAN. I'm sorry but once something has been defrosted it cannot be refrozen.

HEAD. C'mon. Throw me a bone here.

WOMAN. It is a marvelous life. The present. There are wonders. And I shouldn't be telling you this but your partner is only a year or so away from retirement. She is already a national treasure. She is extremely popular.

HEAD. Wrestling and popularity. This isn't the future, this is where I went to high school.

WOMAN. You are being given a great opportunity. Heads in retirement have gone on to sensational careers in punditry, documentary image and alternative music.

HEAD. No.

WOMAN. There is one other option.

HEAD. Yes?

WOMAN. That single red tube connected to your base?

HEAD. What about it?

WOMAN. I could place it in your mouth. You could easily bite through it.

HEAD. And?

WOMAN. And that would be the end.

HEAD. How is this fair? I died young. 38 you said.

WOMAN. Longer than some.

HEAD. You're asking me to spend my second chance at life as a tetherball.

        (The WOMAN *gets up to leave.)*

HEAD. Can I speak to your superior?

WOMAN. No.

HEAD. How about another head?

WOMAN. I'm sorry.

HEAD. Why not?

WOMAN. Yours is a decision that must be made alone. You were right to suggest the future is a bit like high school. But you are amusing. You will catch the eye of the yearbook staff. And your locker is right next to the prom queen.

HEAD. Where are you going?

WOMAN. I have other orientations.

HEAD. Do people die anymore?

WOMAN. Of course.

HEAD. Why? When they can just be revived?

WOMAN. To see what comes next.

HEAD. But it's nothing. I was dead. I know. Nothing comes next.

WOMAN. Makes you think.

(The WOMAN *takes a shiny helmet from her satchel. She places it next to the* HEAD.*)*

WOMAN. Choose life.

(She kisses him on the lips for a while. She then places the red tube in his mouth. The HEAD *holds it delicately between his teeth.)*

WOMAN. Or the only other option.

(She exits.

The HEAD *ponders. He timidly tries to bite through the red tube. He changes his mind. He spits it out.*

There is a great roar and a cheer.

The stage goes black.

The lights come back up on the WOMAN, *dressed ferociously for a wrestling match.*

The HEAD *is tucked under her arm, wearing his helmet, looking equally ferocious. Teeth bared.*

It is like a still photograph. Or a poster. A camera flashes.

Blackout.

Ecstatic cheers.)

End of Play

DAMAGED GOODS
by David Marshall Grant

BIOGRAPHY

As an actor Mr. Grant has starred on Broadway in *Bent*, with Richard Gere, *The Three Sisters*, directed by Scott Elliot and *Angels in America*, for which he was nominated for a Tony award. Film credits include, *American Flyers, Bat 21, Air America, The Chamber, Strictly Business, The Rock, The Stepford Wives*, and *The Devil Wears Prada*. Television credits include, *And The Band Played On*, Russell on *Thirty Something*, and episodes of *Law and Order, CSI Miami, Numbers*, and *Alias*. His first play, *Snakebit*, was nominated for a Drama Desk Award, an Outer Critics Circle Award and was on *Time* magazine's list of the top ten plays of 1999. Other plays include *Current Events*, first produced at The Manhattan Theatre Club, and *Pen*, which had it's world premier at Playwrights Horizons. He is currently a writer/producer on ABC's *Brothers & Sisters*.

ACKNOWLEDGMENTS

Damaged Goods was first produced by Naked Angels at Greenwich Street Theater in New York City as a part of *Fear* (February 13–March 2, 2003). It was directed by Geoffrey Nauffts with the following cast:

KATHLEEN .... Amy Irving
DANIEL.. Peter Frechette

And the following production staff:

Producer..Sherri Kotimsky
Set Design.. Asaki Oda
Lighting Design ....Peter Hoerburger
Costume Design ....Brad Scoggins
Sound Design..A. Stanley Gurczak
Original Music..Rick Baitz

CAST OF CHARACTERS

KATHLEEN
DANIEL

DAMAGED GOODS

The back porch of a house in the Hamptons. A Friday evening in November, 2001.

A bird chirps.

DANIEL, 40s, sits on a white Adirondack chair. He wears jeans and an old sweatshirt. A moment…

KATHLEEN, same age, comes out from inside the house. She's wearing a jacket and gloves and carries a briefcase and an overnight bag.

KATHLEEN. There you are.

DANIEL. Hi.

KATHLEEN. It's a little cold out here, isn't it?

DANIEL. I like it. How was the traffic?

KATHLEEN. A nightmare. It's always a nightmare coming out here. I got into a fight with a man on the Jitney. I was whispering into my cell phone and he—

DANIEL. —You're not supposed to do—

KATHLEEN. I know, but I was whispering. People were talking to each other much louder than I was whispering. It's a stupid rule. It's like jaywalking.

DANIEL. Did you tell him all this?

KATHLEEN. I did actually. I never shut up about it. Poor guy. If he had just let me make one little call.

(DANIEL can't help but laugh.)

It's nice to see you smile.

DANIEL. How was your week?

KATHLEEN. Awful.

DANIEL. It must be quite a busy time for a think tank.

KATHLEEN. Yeah. There's a lot to think about.

(Beat.)

I brought your mail.

DANIEL. Thank you.

(DANIEL takes the mail. He starts to flip through it.)

KATHLEEN. You want my gloves? They're not rubber, but…

(DANIEL gives her a look.)

I was kidding.

(Beat.)

Adam called.

DANIEL. I know. I spoke to him.

KATHLEEN. Adam called me, Daniel.

DANIEL. Oh.

(Putting the mail down:)

You want some wine?

(DANIEL heads inside. KATHLEEN talks louder to be heard.)

KATHLEEN. He's worried about you.

DANIEL. *(Off-Stage:)* You want some goat cheese?

KATHLEEN. No.

(Looking around:)

Did you paint the porch?

DANIEL. *(Off-Stage:)* Yes.

KATHLEEN. Is that like painting the hallway yellow?

(No response.)

Yellow. That was so wrong. At least this is white. I hope you sanded it first.

(No response.)

I've been going after Ashcroft. Did you hear him today?

DANIEL. *(Off-Stage:)* I try to avoid Ashcroft.

KATHLEEN. He's refusing to release the names of more than two-hundred detainees.

(DANIEL comes out with a bottle of wine, glasses, a box of crackers and a hunk of cheese, no tray, and drops them on a table.)

He wants to be able to indefinitely incarcerate U.S. Citizens and summarily strip them of their constitutional rights.

DANIEL. I only have some shitty chardonnay. Sorry.

KATHLEEN. He's basically encouraging citizens to accept autocratic rule as their only way of avoiding terrorism.

DANIEL. You should have thought of all this before you voted for Ralph Nader.

KATHLEEN. You're becoming an alcoholic, you know that.

DANIEL. Actually, I'm merely a wino.

(He hands her a glass of wine.)

KATHLEEN. And by the way, it wouldn't have been any different with Gore.

DANIEL. That was always your argument.

KATHLEEN. My what?

DANIEL. Nothing.

KATHLEEN. I hate when you mumble.

(KATHLEEN *gets some cheese.*)

DANIEL. What did Adam say?

KATHLEEN. What do you think he said? You're not coming to work. The Slim Fast account is going to shit. He said they missed you.

DANIEL. Maybe no one's worrying about dieting right now.

KATHLEEN. Daniel.

DANIEL. Kathy.

KATHLEEN. I miss you, too.

(*Beat.*)

I can't believe how crowded it is out here. I mean, it's November for Christ's sake. I guess you're not the only one.

DANIEL. The only one?

KATHLEEN. Who's still here. Two months after Labor Day.

(*Beat.*)

People are scared, I understand. You're scared. I didn't mean to make that crack about the gloves. And by the way, I think the anthrax is coming from this country. Probably from white supremacists. But this is not the time to dig a hole. That's just what Ashcroft wants you to do so no one notices as we walk away from international agreements willy nilly, our environmental laws are being savaged, our personal liberties trampled on… Look, it's horrible what happened. Horrible. I knew people in that building. We knew people. But no one ever talks about the 200,000 deaths in East Timor brought about by the Indonesian government but inspired and supported by the CIA—

DANIEL. Relax. You're working yourself into a lather.

KATHLEEN. People knew them, too.

(*The bird chirps.*)

Christ.

(*As the bird keeps chirping,* KATHLEEN *reaches into her purse, searching frantically for her cell phone.*)

DANIEL. It's a bird.

KATHLEEN. Sorry, I should get this. I have a piece due on Monday and—

DANIEL. —It's a bird.

(She finally finds the cell phone. It's not ringing.)

KATHLEEN. God…you're right.

(Off the bird's chirping:)

That is totally my ring tone.

DANIEL. Actually, I think it's a Warbling female Tern.

KATHLEEN. She makes the exact same sound as my phone. Really. Call me.

DANIEL. No.

KATHLEEN. Fine. Hold on.

(Playing with the phone:)

Function, menu. Here. Ring Style.

(The cell phone, sounding just like the bird, rings. The bird calls back.)

Am I lying?

(She makes it ring again. The bird answers again. This keeps going, back and forth, for a while.)

DANIEL. What if she thinks your phone is her mother telling her to come home for dinner?

KATHLEEN. Do we have enough food?

DANIEL. Did you know baby monkeys when they're separated from their mothers become so traumatized they end up hugging their feeding device.

KATHLEEN. I would have preferred a feeding device to my mother. At least it would have been consistent.

(Beat.)

Oh, well. I think she's gone.

DANIEL. Off to find her real mother, I'm sure.

KATHLEEN. Lucky bird.

(Silence.)

DANIEL. I was thinking we should eat out tonight. Is that alright with you?

KATHLEEN. Let me take you back to the city. Let's have a meal at Teddy's. It just re-opened.

DANIEL. Kathy…

KATHLEEN. Everyone's scared. I'm scared. And I understand how traumatic this was for you, but it could have been worse… We weren't there. We weren't in the city that day. And I don't want to minimize your feelings, but you're risking your whole career at this point. Adam made it clear to me—

DANIEL. Why does that bother you?

KATHLEEN. Stop mumbling.

DANIEL. I thought you hated my career.

KATHLEEN. I hate parts of your career.

DANIEL. You hate the parts where I try to sell things to people. I'm an ad man. What's left?

KATHLEEN. The creative part.

DANIEL. It's all in service of a strategic message.

KATHLEEN. I want you to come home, Daniel. What else do I have to say? I can't pretend we're not... We're breaking up, Daniel. Do you know that? We're breaking up.

(Beat.)

I wonder if Al-Qaeda's going to take credit for that, too?

(Silence.)

DANIEL. Some people don't consider how I talk mumbling, you know.

KATHLEEN. What?

DANIEL. A woman at work once told me she thought I was soft spoken. Which she went on to say she really liked.

KATHLEEN. However you want to put it, I can't hear you sometimes.

DANIEL. It's just not a big problem anywhere else in my life. No one's ever told me that but you.

KATHLEEN. Occasionally I can't hear you. Forget it. I'll get my ears checked.

DANIEL. I just mean... One man's mumble is another man's—

KATHLEEN. —Gary Cooper. I know, I understand—

DANIEL. —I'm just saying—

KATHLEEN. —And I don't ever give you shit about your career. I was upset once because you were working on a Kraft...whatever it was—

DANIEL. —Macaroni and cheese.

KATHLEEN. Macaroni and cheese. And Kraft is owned by Phillip Morris.

DANIEL. It's separately traded.

KATHLEEN. Whatever.

DANIEL. It makes a difference.

KATHLEEN. It's a cigarette company.

DANIEL. I don't want to get into this again.

KATHLEEN. I don't either.

(Beat.)

I'm sorry, alright. Sometimes I can't let things go. But it's not like I'm being petty. These are issues that matter to me. It's not like I believe in God. I mean, these are my values. It's how I know I'm alive. How I connect. And when the world is about to come apart at the seams... I would think you could understand this a little bit... I would hope you and I could come together. Other people, they're connecting. They're seeing how much they have and they're cherishing it. If I have to listen to a dim-witted east coast preppy turned good old boy tell me the only response to all this is to bomb people the least you can do is let me share my outrage with you. And by the way, we're not going to stop at Afghanistan. Iraq is next, mark my words. We're going to bomb anyone and everyone who isn't "on our side," without once thinking about how we might have contributed to all this. Without once taking responsibility for—

DANIEL. —Actually, I think it's a pretty complicated question what we're responsible for.

KATHLEEN. For God's sake, Daniel, we created Osama Bin Laden. Our support for fascist middle eastern—

DANIEL. —I'm sure his parents had something to do with it, don't you?

KATHLEEN. Why are you being like this?

DANIEL. I'm just saying even though we made a lot of mistakes, less than most I bet, but still mistakes, it doesn't mean he's not a sociopathic religious fundamentalist who would like nothing more than to see you and I burn in hell. And there's a legion of these people following lock-step behind him. I mean, we have our problems but, you know, just because you're paranoid, doesn't mean they're not out to get you.

KATHLEEN. You're being completely ridiculous. Obviously we're culpable. The only way to stop him is to understand that.

(DANIEL starts to head inside.)

Where are you going?

DANIEL. Inside. Is that ridiculous, too?

KATHLEEN. No. It's freezing. The only reason we're out here is because of you.

(She starts to gather her stuff. DANIEL watches her.)

DANIEL. When I was in elementary school there was this kid named Billy Krugman. His father was a asshole. I don't think he hit him, but... Anyway, Billy always felt like a failure. So at school, well, he took it out on me. During recess. To this day that word fills me with dread. Recess. Luckily we were only out there half an hour a day or it would have turned into "Lord of the Flies"—

KATHLEEN. —Are we going inside?

DANIEL. But still, Billy took advantage of every unsupervised minute. My favorite memory is being placed inside the bars of the jungle gym and kept there by a gang of boys while Billy Krugman climbed to the top and spat on me.

KATHLEEN. Jesus.

DANIEL. It wasn't that bad. I never got physically hurt. Just wet. I was terrorized don't get me wrong…but it could have been worse. Mind you, I never fought back. For years I just let this happen. I don't know why. I felt scared. Anyway, one day a bunch of kids took pity on me. They grabbed Billy by the arms and brought him over to me. He was squirming, trying to get away from their grip. One of the kids, Rudy Rolnick, he said, "hit him." "Hit him." They were holding him out for me. They wanted me to put an end to his reign, I guess. And you'll be pleased to know, I wouldn't do it. I wouldn't take a swing. I wish I could tell you it was for some noble reason, my values…but I think I was just scared. When they let go of him, do you know what he did? Billy Krugman punched me in the face.

KATHLEEN. Clearly he needed help.

DANIEL. So did I.

KATHLEEN. He should have been in counseling.

DANIEL. What if he was beyond all that? What if he was damaged goods?

KATHLEEN. Danny, he was ten or something. I'm sure he was salvageable.

DANIEL. What if he wasn't? I was being spat on.

KATHLEEN. Well, where were the teachers?

DANIEL. Exactly. Where were the teachers? They should have stopped him. Sometimes people have to be stopped.

KATHLEEN. Can we please go inside? This is a silly argument.

DANIEL. THESE ARE MY THOUGHTS! GOD DAMN IT, LET ME HAVE MY THOUGHTS! THEY'RE NOT SILLY!

KATHLEEN. I'm sorry.

(Beat.)

Honey, I don't know what you're trying to say.

(Silence.)

DANIEL. It wasn't wrong to paint the hallway yellow. It was my idea, and you didn't like it, but that doesn't make it wrong. But you don't let go. You push it and push it. You keep going and you won't be stopped until I paint it white again. I don't know how to deal with you. You're a bully. I will not be punched in the face again, Kathy. Sometimes I want you to shut up so badly I think of killing you. I don't know any other way to make you stop.

KATHLEEN. You're scaring me.

DANIEL. Good. Maybe you'll listen then.

(Kathleen's cell phone rings. After a few rings she answers it.)

KATHLEEN. *(Into the phone:)* Hello... When... Okay... Let me see if I can get online.

(She hangs up.)

They just blew up five subway cars.

(Silence.)

You can kill me if you think it'll help.

(The bird chirps again.)

(Fade to black.)

End of Play

democracy

TO BE HUMAN
A PLAY FOR TWO GUYS

by Stephen Belber

Playscripts, Inc.
website: www.playscripts.com
email: info@playscripts.com
phone: 1-866-NEW-PLAY (639-7529)

Inquiries concerning all other rights should be addressed to the author's agent: John Buzzetti, The Gersh Agency, 41 Madison Avenue, 33rd floor, New York, NY 10010.

BIOGRAPHY

Stephen Belber's plays include *Geometry of Fire*, (Rattlestick Playwrights Theater); *Fault Lines*, (Naked Angels/Cherry Lane); *A Small, Melodramatic Story*, (LAByrinth Theater Company); *McReele*, (Roundabout); *Match*, (Broadway, Tony nomination for Frank Langella); *Tape*, (Naked Angels, NYC/LA/London); *The Laramie Project*, (Associate Writer); *Carol Mulroney*, (Huntington Theater); *One Million Butterflies*, (Primary Stages); *Drifting Elegant*, (Magic Theater); *The Transparency of Val*, (Theater Outrageous, NYC); *The Wake*, (Via Theater, NYC); *Through Fred*, (Soho Rep); and *The Death of Frank*, (Araca Group, NYC). As a screenwriter, he wrote *Tape*, directed by Richard Linklater, starring Uma Thurman and Ethan Hawke (Sundance; Berlin); *The Laramie Project* (Associate Writer) for HBO Films, (Sundance, Emmy nomination for screenwriting); and *Drifting Elegant*, directed by Amy Glazer. He also wrote and directed his first feature, *Management*, starring Jennifer Aniston, Steve Zahn and Woody Harrelson, which premiered at the 2008 Toronto Film Festival and was released spring 2009. Among other projects, he is currently developing a screenplay based on *McReele*, for Will Smith's Overbrook production company. TV credits include *Rescue Me* and *Law & Order SVU*, (staff writer). He has received commissions from Manhattan Theater Club, Playwrights Horizons, The Huntington Theater, Arena Stage and Philadelphia Theater Company.

ACKNOWLEDGMENTS

To Be Human was first produced by Naked Angels at The Culture Project in New York City as a part of *Democracy* (September 14–October 2, 2004). It was directed by Lucie Tiberghien with the following cast:

JIM ....Stephen Belber
BOB ....Dominic Fumusa

And the following production staff:

Artistic Director of the Evening ....Pippin Parker
Co-Artistic Director of the Evening ....Frank Pugliese
Talent Impresario ....Bruce MacVittie
Producer..Alicia Arinella
Consulting Producer ....Tamlyn Fruend
Associate Producers .... Marin Gazzaniga, Joffre Myers,
Mary Elizabeth Peters
Set Design..Diana Whitten
Lighting Design .... David Szlasa
Costume Design .... Jessica Jahn
Sound Design..Peter Michael Garcia

TO BE HUMAN

A politician named JIM, *at a pulpit, comes to the end of his speech; he speaks with honest integrity.*

JIM. And the *fact* is that I love this country. I think we all do. And I'll tell you something else: It's our *hate* that proves our love. Our *right* to hate, our right to voice that hate with the passion that fuels all love. And I know you've heard that before. And I know you're sitting there right now thinking that politics is a fool's game. That compromise is endemic and so why should you take what we politicians say at face value. And it's true. Nothing of what we say is what it is, and so when a guy like me goes off about "love of country" and "love driving hate" and "I criticize because I care"—that you all have every right to assume that I'm full of it, that it's all just calculated rhetoric—that all it is is layer after layer of lies and deceit. *(Beat.)* And let's just say it is. Let's just say I wrote this speech two years ago, and that today is the 300th time I'm reciting it, and that as I speak I'm thinking about my daughter's SAT scores, and that the reality is that I don't even *have* a daughter and that if I did and if she was at the age where she'd be taking her SATs, then you all could have me arrested——let's just say that all that untruth is *true*. OK then; if that's the case, then my challenge to you today is: How in the world do we get past that, or beyond it, or, perhaps most appropriately, *through* it. How do we actually *celebrate* what we love and *fix* what we hate? Well…if I have an answer, it's this: Let's just try to believe again. Let's *care* enough to believe again. Let's take a leap of faith and fly away towards passion. And my request is that you begin with me. Believe in me, people. Believe that I believe what I'm saying. Believe that I will do what I say. Believe that I'm in this because I wake up each day wanting to make things better. Believe that my hate is love and that my love is cautious. That it's not blind, that it's always with an eye towards improvement. Like a marriage or a good meal or a friendship or a night of bowling: We can always do better. There are always ways for the passion to be perfected. There is always hope that the image of society that we all have stored away in the back of our minds is somehow, perhaps only momentarily, but is somehow, potentially, palpably *attainable*. *(Pause.)* Give me your vote, people, in this fool's game of fools, and I will, in return, hurdle the rhetoric, I will shed the compromise and I will act my heart. I will govern with my soul. I will seek truth where we now least expect to find it. I will *care*. *(Pause.)* Because politics *does* go that deep. Because it is *not* a lost cause. Because it is, in fact, the only tool we have with which to realize a better world. Thank you.

(BOB enters; the crowd dies away.)

BOB. Nice.

JIM. Thanks.

BOB. I think it worked.

JIM. It felt good.

BOB. It feel real?

JIM. It *was* real.

BOB. It was real, no doubt; I could feel it.

JIM. Good—

BOB. Right—

JIM. Good. *(Pause.)* I liked the SAT stuff.

BOB. Thanks—

JIM. Good addition. It felt right.

BOB. Yeah—you know— Acknowledge the Machiavellian, own it, disown it, move on.

JIM. Totally.

BOB. Good.

JIM. Which isn't to say I don't—

BOB. Mean it—

JIM. Totally—

BOB. Because you do.

JIM. I do—

BOB. I know you do. I wrote the shit—I know—you mean it.

JIM. Exactly.

BOB. Good.

JIM. *(Pause.)* What's next?

BOB. *(Off notes:)* Ah—Cleveland.

JIM. Fucking Cleveland.

BOB. I know, but…

JIM. I fucking hate Cleveland. Town of fools. Take everything you say at face value.

> *(They smile at their own joke…)*

JIM. But seriously: Nice job, Bob. You're a good writer.

BOB. Thanks, Jim.

JIM. *(Pause.)* Should we get outta here?

BOB. Sure.

> *(They turn to go. "*JIM*" peels off and around, calls out to* BOB.*)*

ROB. Bob!

BOB. Rob.

ROB. Can I get a quick word?

BOB. Sure.

ROB. Ah——good stuff.

BOB. Yeah?

ROB. Sure.

BOB. Was it what you wanted?

ROB. Ahhh…yeah; basically.

BOB. Good.

ROB. I mean, I think you guys might be playing it just a *little* bit obvious in terms of the duplicity stuff, the whole Machiavelli section.

BOB. A bit much?

ROB. Just a bit.

BOB. Well, no offense, Rob, but it's what you wrote; I mean, it's a *play,* right? —So all we're doing is *playing* the words you wrote.

ROB. *(Reticent:)* Yeah, I know, I was just, I'm always just hoping for, you know, subtlety, in terms of the performance.

BOB. You're saying I'm not subtle.

ROB. I'm not saying you're not subtle, I'm just saying that there were some occasional non-subtle aspects in the version that I just saw, in terms of the sort of "sneaky politician" stuff.

BOB. Fine but then you're more talking about the stuff that Roger was doing, in terms of all the "totally" shit—because he was totally playing that shit for laughs; even though he's just saying the words you wrote.

ROB. I understand—

BOB. You can't fucking control *every* aspect of *every* word you write; if you wanna do that, then just write yourself a part next time.

ROB. How do you know I haven't? I could be fucking acting it out right *now*—making an underlying uber-point about politicians as actors and play-wrights as fledgling warriors attempting to make a difference in a linguistic hall of mirrors.

BOB. Well then I'd say your play sucks, Rob, and that you need a new fuck-ing casting agent when it comes to casting your*self.*

> *(Beat; the two men stare each other down a moment, before "BOB" snaps out of character and addresses "ROB.")*

TIM. OK, let me stop you here for a second. Doug, when Bob comes at you with that last line here, as the playwright I think you're gonna be very shocked, first on just a very *human* level, but *also* shocked *as a playwright,* due to this sort of inherent hubris that playwrights inevitably have. Which I think might force you to respond a bit more viscerally, maybe some blood to the face, some vein-popping on the forehead, I dunno—whatever it is you think you can come up with there.

DOUG. *(Very simple:)* I've never seen *you* pop veins in your forehead, Tim.

TIM. I know, I know, but that's because I'm a pretty level-headed play-wright, but some of these guys, it's incredible, the vanity affects their veins in ways you can't imagine. That's a play on words, isn't it, vain, vanity, vein—-excellent. Anyway, I just wanna make sure you don't *under*play it because I think the humor there will come from the sort of heroic-pathetic playwright pleading for subtlety in the most unsubtle of ways.

DOUG. I thought playwrights weren't supposed to direct their own plays.

TIM. It's true, it's true, I just didn't want anyone to fuck this one up. But you're right, maybe I shouldn't have *cast* it. I'm kidding, that's not a jab at you. *(To off-stage:)* OK—can we move on to the next scene!

> *(As* TIM *turns away,* "DOUG" *gently taps him on the shoulder, reluctantly interrupting:)*

RON. Ah, Tim, can I just, umm, can I just make a quick comment?

TIM. Ah—sure.

RON. It's completely unsolicited, so if it rings true, that's great, and if not, I completely understand—

TIM. No it's fine, it's what you're here for, fire away.

RON. Well, it's just that I've been noticing that…well—no—actually, let me phrase it this way: What's the actual point of what you're trying to say here?

TIM. "Here"?

RON. With this play.

TIM. What kind of question is that?

RON. Umm, it's a, I guess, I dunno, a dramaturgical one?

TIM. Right, of course. It's what you're here for.

RON. I mean, that's what—

TIM. No, it is, I'm sorry, I get testy sometimes—

RON. It's completely understandable.

TIM. I think the *point,* Ron, is that politics is, it's a very tricky business.

RON. OK.

TIM. And that it's very hard to get at what you think you're trying to get at.

RON. Absolutely.

TIM. And that if there's such a thing as a political truth, it probably has something to do with the fact that truth really only occurs when, when the lies stop. You see what I'm saying?

RON. Ah—can you elaborate a bit?

TIM. Sure, sure. Truth is...let me see if I can state this the way I feel it: Truth is a lack of lies.

RON. OK.

TIM. Actually—truth is a *pack* of lies, that eventually gets unwrapped.

RON. So it's a pack that's *wrapped?*

TIM. Yes—it's a pack that's *wrapped,* that eventually gets *un*wrapped, and you take out all those lies, lie after lie, and if you're lucky, *very* lucky, then there's occasionally a kernel of *truth* down there, at the bottom of the box—

RON. The pack—

TIM. The pack—yes; there's a kernel of *truth* at the bottom of the *pack,* and if we hold that truth up, and acknowledge it for the survivor that it is, the cockroach at the cessation of the nuclear fallout, and if we can manage to cast a *vote* for that cockroach, then maybe, just maybe, we can begin to get back to the base values and political instincts upon which this nation was founded. Which were good instincts; which were, after all, *enlightened,* instincts, having to do with human *being,* with an essential human *attitude* that, if applied in the context of the here and now of today's world, would be incredibly helpful in finding our way in this lost time. If we had an attitude that could instantly recall what it is to be *human.* If we had that, I do think we'd be in much better shape.

RON. *(Beat.)* Because the thing is——which is why I bring this up—I think that what my friend was looking for was something a little less...I dunno——*beclouded* by political platitude, and maybe just more honest. I mean, his whole camp is really looking for something honest, and probably just more simple.

TIM. Well then he shouldn't have asked a fucking playwright. We're not simple beings. We're actually incredibly complex, and that complexity is exactly what playwrights attempt to take on each and every outing.

RON. OK. *(Pause.)* I'll let him know.

("TIM" does a 360 and calls out to RON:*)*

BILL. Hey, Ron, what's up with the fucking play we ordered?

RON. Oh, hey, man. Yeah, they're still working on it.

BILL. Dude, it was supposed to be ready already.

RON. I know, Tim's having some trouble ironing out his message.

BILL. Well what's his unifying principle?

RON. I'm not sure he has one yet, Bill. He's still sort of searching for it.

BILL. He's floundering?— The fucking guy's floundering?

RON. I would say he's floundering a bit, yes. But I mean that's kind of the way he works.

BILL. Well it's total bullshit, amigo. The thing's in three days and his thing's supposed to be the centerpieces of the whole fucking thing.

RON. We're working on it.

BILL. You're a fucking dramaturg, amiga—fucking dramaturg that shit.

RON. I'm working on it—

BILL. Good, 'cause Jim is psyched but he doesn't want bullshit. He wants like a classical, revolutionary, *audacious* motherfucking piece of theater. He doesn't want fucking street theater, dude, he wants the motherfucking mother of all motherfucking plays.

RON. We're working on it.

BILL. Good.

RON. *(Pause.)* Like maybe even with you as a character?

BILL. *(As it dawns on him...)* Shut up.

RON. I'm serious—

BILL. Shut up—

RON. I'm serious—

BILL. Shut up—

RON. I'm serious.

BILL. Like *this* might be part of the play?

RON. Yeah.

BILL. *This* conversation?

RON. Yeah—

BILL. Like *I* might be a fucking character?

RON. Yeah.

BILL. *In* the motherfucking play?

RON. Yeah.

BILL. Like a play within a play within a play within the fucking thing?

RON. Yeah.

BILL. *(Pause.)* I FUCKING LOVE THAT SHIT, DUDE!!! I FUCKING

LOVE THAT SHIT.

RON. Me too.

BILL. You're like a fucking genius.

RON. It's actually been done a lot.

BILL. I don't care, man, I *never* go to fucking theater so it's a fucking whole new fucking ball game, dude!

RON. I'm glad you like it.

BILL. I gotta go fucking tell Jim!

RON. OK, then, I'll see you later.

BILL. *(To "DOUG":) JIM!!!*

JIM. Yeah?

BILL. You're never gonna fucking believe this!

JIM. Let me suspend my disbelief.

BILL. Those fucking theater guys that you asked me to ask to do a fucking theater thing for us—?

JIM. Yeah?

BILL. Well they did a play!

JIM. Ah huh.

BILL. And it's almost done!

JIM. Yeah.

BILL. And guess the fuck what? We're *IN* the motherfucking thing!

JIM. We're in the play?

BILL. We're in the motherfucking play, amigo!! We're *in* the fucking thing!

JIM. *(Beat.)* Do we have good parts?

BILL. Totally, man. *We're* the guys with integrity and the *theater guys* are the fucking bozos!

JIM. Seriously?

BILL. Seriously! *(Pause.)* I *think.*

JIM. *(Pause.)* Cool. *(Beat.)* Integrity like…like *how?*

BILL. *(Beat.)* Umm. Maybe not *integrity,* but definitely like, the last word on it all.

JIM. Like the end of the play?

BILL. Totally. Like the end of the play.

JIM. What do we say?

BILL. You get to end your speech.

JIM. What speech?

BILL. The speech you were giving at the beginning; the speech that Bob wrote for you.

JIM. Bob?

BILL. Bob the speechwriter. *(Beat.)* He looked like me.

JIM. But you're Bill.

BILL. I know. I'm your fucking policy wonk. *(Pause.)* It's part of the whole thing about how people who work for politicians just sort of fucking blend into each other no matter even who they work for or what party they belong to.

JIM. *(Not:)* Interesting.

BILL. Totally.

JIM. So how do I end my speech?

BILL. You get to talk about cutting through the bullshit and believing in what you say.

JIM. Cool. *(Pause.)* So *what* do I get to say that I believe in?

BILL. *(Pause.)* You talk about how it's not too late.

JIM. Too late for what?

BILL. How it's not too late to care. To cut through the billion layers of bullshit and care. How it's easier *not* to care, but that if we get up off our asses, we still might find something to care in.

JIM. It sounds a little bland, Bill.

BILL. It's totally bland.

JIM. It's totally bland.

BILL. But it's true, right? It's fucking true. All we have to do is get off our ass and care.

JIM. All we have to do is get off our ass and care.

BILL. All we have to do is fucking get off our fucking ass and care.

JIM. All we have to do is fucking get off our ass and care.

BILL. All we have to do is fucking care.

JIM. All we have to do is fucking care.

BILL. All we have to do...

JIM. *(Arriving at podium; pause for honest effect:)* All we have to do is care. *(Beat.)* Thank you. Good night.

      (Silence; BILL is proud of JIM; beat.)

BILL. You did it, man. You pulled off the end. Of the "play."

JIM. I know. *(Pause; turning to him:)* I'm the one who wrote it.

End of Play

REAGAN IN HELL
by Lee Blessing

Playscripts, Inc.
website: www.playscripts.com
email: info@playscripts.com
phone: 1-866-NEW-PLAY (639-7529)

Inquiries concerning all other rights should be addressed to the author's agent: Judy Boals, Judy Boals, Inc., 307 West 38th Street, #812, New York, NY 10018.

BIOGRAPHY

Lee Blessing's *A Walk in the Woods* appeared on Broadway and in London's West End. His Off-Broadway credits include: *Eleemosynary, Cobb, Thief River, Chesapeake* and *Down the Road*—plus *Fortinbras, Lake Street Extension, Two Rooms,* and the world premiere of *Patient A,* all in the 1992–93 Signature Theatre Season. Recent regional productions include *Whores* at the Contemporary American Theater Festival and *Black Sheep* at Florida Stage and Barrington Stage. Other plays include *Going to St. Ives, Independence, Riches, Oldtimers Game,* and *Nice People Dancing to Country Music.* Awards include: The American Theatre Critics Association Award, the L.A. Drama Critics Award, the Great American Play Award, the Humanitas Award, and the George and Elisabeth Marton Award, among others. His plays have been nominated for Tony and Olivier Awards, as well as for the Pulitzer Prize. Mr. Blessing is the author of over twenty plays and screenplays. He currently resides in New York City.

ACKNOWLEDGMENTS

Reagan in Hell was first produced by Naked Angels at The Culture Project in New York City as a part of *Democracy* (September 14–October 2, 2004). It was directed by Daniel Goldstein with the following cast:

CLARK .... Robert Sella
REAGAN .... Frank Raiter

And the following production staff:

Artistic Director of the Evening .... Pippin Parker
Co-Artistic Director of the Evening .... Frank Pugliese
Talent Impresario .... Bruce MacVittie
Producer .... Alicia Arinella
Consulting Producer .... Tamlyn Fruend
Associate Producers .... Marin Gazzaniga, Joffre Myers,
Mary Elizabeth Peters
Set Design .... Diana Whitten
Lighting Design .... David Szlasa
Costume Design .... Jessica Jahn
Sound Design .... Peter Michael Garcia

CAST OF CHARACTERS

CLARK
REAGAN

REAGAN IN HELL

> CLARK, *a demon, at a desk. Phone rings.*

CLARK. Hell. Alzheimer's Division. What? No, it's coming right up.

> *(Consulting his clipboard:)*

Next on the list. Yeah, yeah—I'll let you know how it goes.

> *(Hanging up:)*

Fucking imps.

> *(Suddenly screaming in a terrifying, otherworldly voice—which will always be designated by caps and bolds:)*

NEXT!!!

> *(RONALD REAGAN enters. CLARK instantly resumes his pleasant, helpful demeanor:)*

Hi, there. Have a seat.

> *(As REAGAN, confused, remains standing:)*

Go ahead and have a seat.

> *(No response.)*

The chair. Right behind you.

> *(No response.)*

Just sit down, and we'll get started.

> *(No response—remaining polite and cheerful:)*

Sit.

> *(No response.)*

Sit.

> *(No response.)*

Down.

> *(No response.)*

Down, boy. C'mon!

> *(No response.)*

Just fold in the middle there.

> *(No response.)*

You remember sitting.

> *(No response.)*

Sixty-one percent of a human life. Sitting.

> *(No response.)*

Big favorite.

(No response.)

Sit for me? I'm here to help.

(No response.)

No help for the standing.

(No response.)

Dutch? Dutch, baby—you in there?

(No response.)

Mr. President?

(No response.)

Anybody home.

(No response—sighing:)

I've got the worst fucking job in Hell.

(CLARK goes to REAGAN, stands toe to toe with him and places his middle finger against REAGAN's forehead. He pushes REAGAN gently until REAGAN is more or less obliged to sit or fall over. REAGAN sits.)

DO NOT GET UP UNTIL I TELL YOU TO!!!

(Returning to his clipboard, speaking in a bored, rote, done-it-a-billion-times tone:)

Welcome to Hell, Alzheimer's Division. You are here because you're a victim of Alzheimer's. Remember that. At the Gates of Hell you were informed of the nature of the evil impulses to which you succumbed in life and the perfidious acts by which you caused the suffering of untold numbers of others. This should have occurred while Cerberus the three-headed dog was rending your flesh.

(CLARK checks REAGAN's ankles by lifting his pant legs. The ankles are very bloody. CLARK checks off a box on his clipboard list.)

Good. Why we in Hell choose to punish humans for causing suffering—when we demons take so much pride in the suffering we ourselves cause—is a philosophical dilemma with which you will not concern yourself. *IS THAT CLEAR?!!!*

REAGAN. Mommy?

CLARK. 1 ain't your mommy.

REAGAN. Mommy?

CLARK. Your mommy isn't here. The following are the Rules of Hell/Alzheimer's Division. You will remember them. If you do not remember them, you will be *SEVERELY PUNISHED!* Is that clear?

REAGAN. Mommy?

CLARK. Why do you think your mommy's here?

REAGAN. Mommy?

CLARK. *(Indicating the thickness of the papers on his clipboard:)* You are not going to blame all this on your mommy, believe me. Rule Number One: Remember These Rules. Rule Number Two: You are entitled to a list of the Torments of Hell to which you will be subjected. You are entitled to this not because you have any rights whatsoever but because Satan views it as just one more Torment. First Torment: You have advanced AIDS. There is no treatment for AIDS in Hell. You will suffer from this condition for eternity.

REAGAN. Mommy?

CLARK. Second Torment: While in Hell your job will be to sit in that chair taking an eternal shower in the burning shit and vomit of most of the Salvadoran army of the 1980s, as well as much of the Nicaraguan Contra forces from the same period. They get a big dinner down here, and as you may know the food in Hell is both putrid and *HOT!!!!!*

REAGAN. Mommy?

CLARK. Not in the building, big fella. Third Torment: A copy of the U.S. Constitution, festooned with razor-blades, will be rolled into a flaming baton and *SHOVED UP YOUR FUCKING ASS!!!* You probably thought that razor-blade bit was just something kids think up to scare each other with, but it actually is real. Is all of this clear?

REAGAN. Mommy?

CLARK. What did I just say?

REAGAN. Mommy?

CLARK. Close enough. From now until the Crack of Doom, Oliver North will eat your liver and then vomit it down your throat, where it will regrow and start the cycle all over again. Occasionally he'll vomit into your eyes instead, just for a change of pace, but in any case your liver will grow back again for Ollie's next meal.

REAGAN. This is my microphone.

CLARK. No more microphones for you, Ron. But you will be the official greeter for all the homicidal Central-American generals and politicians you kept in power, plus those in your administration who helped you lie to Congress, subvert the law and perpetuate discrimination against gays. That's your Fourth Torment. Torment Number Five: Several of the right-wing religious leaders whose figurative dicks you sucked are scheduled to arrive shortly and will expect a more literal version of the same activity.

REAGAN. Are there jelly beans?

CLARK. There are no jelly beans in Hell Gipper, sad to say. But for you we're importing an eternal stock of them, so you'll never be without. They taste like Salvadoran children who've been shot and hacked to death by government forces, then buried in mud for twenty years. *Bon appetit!* Not that you'll remember the taste from one jelly bean to the next. Still, I guess that's better since it'll be a surprise each time. Ok—that pretty much sums up how you'll be spending eternity. Oh, there's some good news. We have as it happens a few truly evil people who died of AIDS-related causes during your tenure in office, and they'll drop by to clean all the Salvadoran shit off your head by pissing on you from time to time. So don't tell me there isn't a bright spot. Any questions?

REAGAN. Mommy?

CLARK. Asked and answered. Rule Three: It is imperative that you remember each and every torment you suffer every day. You will be given a daily quiz on them. If you fail it, the torments will automatically double.

REAGAN. Who are you?

CLARK. I'm a *DEMON FROM HELL, RONALD REA—!!!*

(Sighing as he sees it makes no impression.)

Demon from hell. Alzheimer's Division. I'll be your case-worker. I'm in charge of your punishment…and you're in charge of mine.

REAGAN. *(A random, lucid moment:)* What do you mean?

CLARK. *(Surprised:)* Just…I'm the lowest demon in all of Hell, that's all. That's why Satan's got me tormenting those who can't even remember why they're suffering.

REAGAN. *(Gone again:)* Mommy?

CLARK. *(Depressed:)* That's right. Mommy. I'm your mommy, kid. I'm your mommy, and you've been a very bad little boy.

REAGAN. Do I have to stay in?

CLARK. Oh boy, do you have to stay in.

REAGAN. Will someone come over to play?

CLARK. Absolutely. You won't be alone. Everybody who knew better but sang your praises anyway when you died? They're all be here. They knew what you'd done, but they wouldn't put one word of it into the media, can you imagine that? All because it was an election year. Oh, yeah—they're all going to hell. And compared to them, you'll have it easy. After all, they'll actually know why they're here.

(Grabbing the clipboard:)

Fourth and Final Rule: Be grateful. Because it can always—*ALWAYS—*

GET WORSE!!! Ok, I'd better get out of here before the torments begin. Enjoy your stay in Hell. See you in a millennium.

> (CLARK *exits. Smiling, unaware,* REAGAN *looks up straight above into the light.*)

REAGAN. Mommy?

> (*Blackout.*)

End of Play

THE DYING CITY
by Christopher Shinn

BIOGRAPHY

Christopher Shinn was born in Hartford, Connecticut, and lives in New York. His plays have been premiered by the Royal Court Theatre, Lincoln Center Theater, Manhattan Theatre Club, Playwrights Horizons, the Vineyard Theatre, South Coast Rep, and Soho Theatre, and later seen regionally in the United States and around the world. He is the winner of an OBIE in Playwriting (2004-2005) and a Guggenheim Fellowship in Playwriting (2005), was a Pulitzer Prize finalist (2008), was shortlisted for the Evening Standard Theatre Award for Best Play (2008), and has also been nominated for an Olivier Award for Most Promising Playwright (2003), a TMA Award for Best New Play (2006), a Lucille Lortel Award for Outstanding Play (2007), and a South Bank Show Award for Theatre (2009). In 2009, his adaptation of *Hedda Gabler* premiered on Broadway at the Roundabout (American Airlines Theatre) and he has also written short plays for Naked Angels, the 24 Hour Plays, and the New York International Fringe Festival (2002 winner, Best Overall Production). He has received grants from the NEA/TCG Residency Program and the Peter S. Reed Foundation, and he is a recipient of the Robert S. Chesley Award. He teaches playwriting at the New School for Drama.

ACKNOWLEDGMENTS

The Dying City was first produced by Naked Angels at The Culture Project in New York City as a part of *Democracy* (September 14–October 2, 2004). It was directed by Will Frears with the following cast:

TOM...Jesse Tyler Ferguson
DENISE...Emily Bergl
JERRY...Jordan Bridges

And the following production staff:

Artistic Director of the Evening ....Pippin Parker
Co-Artistic Director of the Evening...................Frank Pugliese
Talent Impresario ....Bruce MacVittie
Producer...Alicia Arinella
Consulting Producer ....Tamlyn Fruend
Associate Producers................. Marin Gazzaniga, Joffre Myers,
                                                          Mary Elizabeth Peters
Set Designer ....Diana Whitten
Lighting Designer..David Szlasa
Costume Designer..Jessica Jahn
Sound Designer ....Peter Michael Garcia

CAST OF CHARACTERS

TOM
DENISE
JERRY

THE DYING CITY

TOM, DENISE, *and* JERRY, *late 20s, in a bar.*

JERRY. But let me just say this: why do Americans have to be perfect. Why are we expected to be perfect.

DENISE. This is fascinating—the question of the superego.

JERRY. I'm not even talking Freudian shit, I'm talking basic level—I'm a little drunk, excuse me—but I mean—okay—well wait, let me go back. I have a friend from high school who's a Captain in Iraq, right, and the thing with this guy, God bless him, he genuinely believes that the military is good, that the American military—the guy knows more history than all three of us at this table times ten, you know, and he wanted to be a part of the military because he honestly believed America's a force for good. But the thing is *now,* is now I get these, these *emails,* he's stationed in Iraq, and he's watching everything go down, and he's bitching about how *stupid* the soldiers in his command are. They don't *know* anything, he goes on and on, they don't *know* anything, they're so *stupid,* they don't know any *history,* they can't speak proper *English,* they can't *think,* they don't have any critical skills and all this. Excuse me: does everyone need to be a genius now all of a sudden? Does every American have to uphold some, you know, some cosmic, some standard of, I mean, you know, aren't we pretty good? I mean aren't we pretty fucking good, you know, we didn't burn anybody in ovens or you know, invade France or, you know, decide to, I mean, yeah, we have faults, but I mean, excuse me, you know?

TOM. So what you're saying / is

JERRY. What I'm saying is, you know, does everyone in America, in the American military have to be a great moral thinker now, you know, I mean, just because we happen to be the most powerful country? Are we supposed to hold up the whole world with our, be better and smarter than everybody else just because—you know?

DENISE. I see what you're saying.

JERRY. The world is blaming us for human nature like we're not supposed to be human! We're not supposed to have stupid people in our country!

DENISE. Look, the world is bleak—that's what you're saying.

JERRY. George Bush didn't cut anybody's ears off—and I voted for Gore, but. I have to piss.

(JERRY exits. Pause.)

DENISE. He has an interesting perspective…

TOM. Yeah…

DENISE. He's kind of—

TOM. No—

DENISE. I'm not saying I agree. I'm not saying he's completely *coherent.*

TOM. No, you know…

DENISE. He makes me feel good.

    (Pause.)

DENISE. I need something till Fred comes back.

TOM. He's—is he—I mean, have you spoken to him?

DENISE. What I mean is, I'm still hopeful he'll change his mind. In the meantime…

TOM. Right.

DENISE. What about you?

TOM. Oh…I had a weird night with Kevin.

DENISE. You did?

TOM. I don't know. He invited me over to watch a movie. And I thought, I had sort of made up my mind he wasn't into me. But then he answered the door, when I went over to his place to watch the movie, he was in his underwear. And I thought—you know?

DENISE. Maybe he just happened to be in his underwear when you arrived.

TOM. I buzzed, he had to buzz me in.

DENISE. Maybe he had been on the phone or something when you buzzed.

    (Pause.)

I'm not—maybe he wanted you to see him in his underwear.

TOM. I don't know. I'm gonna stay away from him I think, I mean it's either he's being provocative or, you know, he's totally in denial about—because he had, on his couch, you know, near where the TV is, he had some lotion, and he made reference to having just masturbated which was why the lotion was out and he said, "Ignore the lotion" as though it was a joke. But I couldn't tell if it was a joke or it was meant to

DENISE. Maybe he forgot the lotion was there and was embarrassed.

TOM. But—he pointed out the lotion.

DENISE. Perhaps he figured you saw the lotion and put two and two together and he felt he had to acknowledge it.

TOM. Well—of course then I got all excited but then we just watched the movie and of course nothing happened, so I am really going to just stay away from him. Because, you know, these actors, what do they think? I don't understand how they

DENISE. I once knew an actor who, when he masturbated, he imagined that he himself had a vagina and was fucking himself.

(*Pause.*)

TOM. Anyway…I guess Kevin and I did have a nice talk about his brother's depression, his brother's on an antipsychotic now, and I talked about my depression and…I don't know—so. Anyway…

(*Pause.*)

DENISE. I think—I know he's somewhat—but I think what Jerry is trying to say is, we need to be gentler with ourselves. More forgiving. We're only human. That goes for me and you and for George Bush too. You know, he didn't fly two planes into those buildings. And some kid in Flint who joins the Army to—everyone is deserving of understanding.

TOM. Yeah, well. What did the Germans say.

DENISE. What do you mean.

TOM. When, you know—six million Jews.

DENISE. I don't think Jerry's saying *that.*

TOM. Oh—you know, we're only human—we can't be expected to not build concentration camps given—

(*JERRY returns.*)

JERRY. Hey.

DENISE. Hello.

JERRY. Man. I've been talking a lot—I was pissing and realized my jaw hurt.

DENISE. It's very interesting, though, what we were talking about. I think people around the world envy America. We're the most powerful country, we

JERRY. Oh, absolutely! Ask any father. Ask any father anywhere, everyone wants something from him, and the father has nobody to go complain to or bitch to. *Absolutely.*

(*Pause.*)

TOM. Well…some fathers, you know, beat their kids or their wives or—you know, my father would come home from work, sometimes he would beat me up for no reason, so. A lot of kids get beat, that's what their fathers do.

JERRY. Right. And sometimes they don't deserve it, right.

TOM. Well—I don't think I ever deserved it.

JERRY. I'm not—we could get into the specifics of one example, I'm not saying every case, I'm saying more generally. In my experience, most kids deserve to get a beating every now and

TOM. Do you have kids?

JERRY. No—my experiences of observation, as well as having been a kid and gotten a few beatings myself.

TOM. Well, I actually don't think anyone deserves to be abused, so.

JERRY. You know, though, who *wasn't* abused? That's like, you know, you get into a weird territory when you start talking about abuse. Would most people say they were abused if they had never heard the word "abuse"?

 (Pause.)

TOM. But there *is* a word "abuse."

 (Pause.)

DENISE. I believe it's inappropriate for people in power to use their power in a way that hurts other people who are less than—who are—but what I think Jerry is saying is, Saddam Hussein is not a child.

JERRY. And, weapons of mass destruction are not toys.

TOM. But there were no weapons of mass destruction.

 (Pause.)

JERRY. You know, when I see these kids protesting here, I wanna say to them, look: if you lived in Iraq they would cut off your thumbs for even *thinking* about protesting. And you're gonna tell these Iraqi twenty-two-year-olds that only American kids should have Diesel jeans and American Spirit Lights, and *they* should live in tyranny for the rest of their lives?

DENISE. I don't think it's so much that the protesters don't think Iraqis should be free—it's that they don't trust George Bush.

JERRY. Yeah, because he's "dumb." Well, there's worse than dumb in this world, I'm sorry to say.

 (Pause.)

DENISE. I was on the subway late at night once, and I got off the train, and I walked towards the exit, and it was one of those revolving door exits, with bars on it, dividing it up so you have your own little compartment when you walk through the exit. And there was a man behind me. And the man, when I went into the exit and began to go through, he pulled on the door and trapped me. He held onto one of the bars and I couldn't push the door, I couldn't get out. No one was around and I asked him to let me go, I begged him to please let me go. He didn't say anything, he just kept holding the door. I think this went on for at least twenty minutes.

JERRY. Jesus.

DENISE. There was nothing he could do to me—there was no way for him to pull the door back, because it only moved forward. He just wanted to trap me for a while and watch me suffer. Finally another train came and he let me go and I ran out of the station. And I was so frightened.

    (Pause.)

It's like the world feels like I did—trapped like that, like America is holding them there, watching them suffer. But they don't understand that we feel trapped too. We're frightened too.

    (Pause. Tom's phone rings. He looks at it. Pause. He answers it.)

TOM. Hello? Hey Kevin. Sure. Okay.

    *(*TOM *hangs up the phone. Pause.)*

That's a friend, I'm probably gonna take off…

    (Pause.)

So. Nice to meet you!

JERRY. Yeah, you too.

    *(*TOM *rises.)*

DENISE. I'll give you a call tomorrow.

TOM. Okay. Bye.

    *(*TOM *starts to go.)*

DENISE. Say hello to Kevin for me.

    *(*TOM *smiles and goes.)*

JERRY. Nice guy.

DENISE. He's very dear to me.

JERRY. I just—why don't people understand they want to kill us? We work so hard, we strive, we build this country…

DENISE. Will you hold me?

JERRY. You wanna go?

DENISE. Yes.

JERRY. What else do you want.

DENISE. I want you to hold me.

JERRY. That it?

DENISE. Take me home.

End of Play

armed
and naked
in america

Natalia Payne and Logan Marshall-Green in *After The Deer Hunter*
Naked Angels at The Duke in New York City (2007).

AFTER THE DEER HUNTER
by Nicole Burdette

Playscripts, Inc.
website: www.playscripts.com
email: info@playscripts.com
phone: 1-866-NEW-PLAY (639-7529)

BIOGRAPHY

Nicole Burdette is a playwright and an actress. She co-founded and named the Naked Angels theater company in 1986, where many of her plays have been produced. *The Bluebird Special Came Through Here* (directed by Rebecca Miller), *Busted* (directed by Timothy Hutton), *Chelsea Walls* (directed by Edwin Sherin) and many others.

Her adaptation of her play *Chelsea Walls* was made into a film, which premiered at the Cannes Film Festival in 2001. As an actress Ms. Burdette has worked with directors Robert Redford, Martin Scorsese, David Lynch, Alan Parker, John Patrick Shanley, Kenneth Lonergan, Matthew Broderick, etc. in both theater and film.

ACKNOWLEDGMENTS

After The Deer Hunter was first produced by Naked Angels at The Duke in New York City as a part of *Armed and Naked in America* (April 11–22, 2007). It was directed by Jodie Markell with the following cast:

NATASHA..Natalia Payne
JOHN...Logan Marshall-Green

And the following production staff:

Producer..Andy Donald, Dan Klores
Scenic Design...David Rockwell
Lighting Design ....Jason Lyons
Costume Design ....Jessica Wegener
Sound Design...........................Drew Levy, Tony Smolenski IV
Projection Design..............Batwin and Robin Productions, Inc.

CAST OF CHARACTERS

NATASHA
JOHN

AFTER THE DEER HUNTER

Lights up on a car parked at night.

The headlights shine. It is a wintry, cold Minnesota night. You could hear a pin drop. Snow is falling soft and slow.

NATASHA, *17, sits in the passenger seat.*

JOHN, *a boy from military school—though dressed in civvies sits behind the wheel.* JOHN *is tall and has short dark hair. He wears a peacoat.*

NATASHA *wears a brown leather bomber jacket with a mink fur collar. Her hair is pulled back like a ballerina.*

Both of these characters have a stoic Midwestern quality to their [minimal] movements, upright posture and their soft spoken toughness. They are beauties and they are way beyond their years.

JOHN *turns off the engine [and the head lights].*

They both stare straight ahead.

After a while JOHN *speaks.*

JOHN. *(Speaks straight up:)* I've never seen a movie like that before.

NATASHA. Me neither.

JOHN. It was so real.

NATASHA. The Russian Roulette…

JOHN. Yeah.

(Long silence.)

NATASHA. When do you go back to school?

JOHN. Monday after Easter.

NATASHA. Do you like military school?

JOHN. No.

NATASHA. But you have to go?

JOHN. Yup.

(Long silence.)

JOHN. Do you go to school with Joan?

NATASHA. No.

JOHN. How come you were at her party?

NATASHA. Her father works with my father.

JOHN. It's just that I never saw you before.

NATASHA. I go to a theater school downtown.

JOHN. Oh.

NATASHA. I'm not around much. I practically lived at my friend Jessica's. Downtown.

JOHN. *(Smiles.)* Well, I'm glad you went to Joan's.

NATASHA. *(Nonplussed:)* Me too.

JOHN. Are you okay?

NATASHA. Uh-huh.

JOHN. You have very sad eyes.

NATASHA. That's not a nice thing to say.

JOHN. It's the truth.

NATASHA. I'm not like those other rich girls.

JOHN. I know. That's why I asked you out.

NATASHA. *(Smiles.)* Why? You wanna see how the other half lives.

JOHN. Which other half?

NATASHA. *(Shrugs.) (Soft:)* Damaged.

JOHN. You're not damaged.

NATASHA. *(Shrugs.) (Sighs soft:)* I don't care.

JOHN. Try going to military school—if you really want to be damaged. That'll do it—real good.

> *(NATASHA looks at JOHN for the first time. He looks down.)*

NATASHA. *(Smiles.)* That's why I went to the movies with you.

> *(JOHN still looks down.)*

JOHN. *(After a while:)* I got something for you.

> *(NATASHA says nothing.*
>
> JOHN *reaches into his inside peacoat pocket and takes out a ribbon medal and a small brass star.)*

Here's some of the stuff they give us at school.

NATASHA. W-will you get in trouble if you give these to me?

JOHN. Nah, it's a ribbon and a brass star. They know we're gonna end up giving them to girls on break anyway. They act pissed off but they know the score —that's how they are about everything. Acting angry, acting proud. *(Shakes his head.)* It's all bullshit.

NATASHA. *(She understands this.)* That's how everyone is.

JOHN. Yeah. But I want you have them. I never gave a girl this stuff before—I never wanted to glorify it, like it mattered—but I want you to have them.

NATASHA. *(She holds on to them.)* Thank you. If you need them back—

JOHN. I won't.

NATASHA. Thank you.

(Another silence occurs. It is less intense this time.

JOHN *reaches over* NATASHA *and opens the glove compartment.)*

JOHN. Pardon me.

(He gets a cassette tape from the glove compartment.)

I want to play you something. It's a bootleg record I got from a kid at school.

(JOHN turns the car back on and puts the cassette in.

Live Bruce Springsteen plays "Darkness On The Edge of Town".

It gets louder and louder.

They both listen [looking ahead] —their emotion simmers with the music [in their stoic Midwestern way].

The music crescendos.

Their emotions simmer more until they kiss—in a passionate clinch the lights go out on the tableau.

Then, the music goes out.)

End of Play

THE BULLY COMPOSITION
by Will Eno

BIOGRAPHY

Will Eno is a Guggenheim Fellow, a Helen Merrill Playwriting Fellow, and a Fellow of the Edward F. Albee Foundation. *The Flu Season* premiered at The Gate Theatre in London and then opened in New York where it won the Oppenheimer Award (2004) for best debut by an American playwright. His play *Thom Pain (based on nothing)* was a finalist for the 2005 Pulitzer Prize in Drama. His collection of short plays *Oh, The Humanity and other good intentions* was produced at the Flea Theater in New York in November 2007. An excerpt of his play *Tragedy: a tragedy* appeared in the June 2006 issue of *Harper's Magazine. Tragedy: a tragedy* had its U.S. premiere at Berkeley Rep Theatre in March of 2008. His plays are published by Oberon Books, in London, and by TCG and Playscripts, in the United States.

ACKNOWLEDGMENTS

The Bully Composition was first produced by Naked Angels at The Duke in New York City as a part of *Armed and Naked in America* (April 11–22, 2007). It was directed by Daniel Aukin with the following cast:

PHOTOGRAPHER .... Thomas Jay Ryan
ASSISTANT .... Elizabeth Marvel

And the following production staff:

Producers .... Andy Donald, Dan Klores
Scenic Design .... David Rockwell
Lighting Design .... Jason Lyons
Costume Design .... Jessica Wegener
Sound Design .... Drew Levy, Tony Smolenski IV
Projection Design .... Batwin and Robin Productions, Inc.

DRAMATIS PERSONAE

PHOTOGRAPHER, male, 30–50

ASSISTANT, female, 30–40

(In the program, no roles should be listed. Only the actors' names should appear, e.g., "John Smith. Jane Jones." The reason for this is to encourage the audience to more easily accept the possibility that this is an improvisation.)

SETTING

Theatre.

STAGE PROPERTIES

A camera (with a flash), a tripod, a light meter, some lights. A folder full of photos and papers.

THE BULLY COMPOSITION

PHOTOGRAPHER *and* ASSISTANT *enter.* PHOTOGRAPHER *begins to set up a camera [with a flash, perhaps some remote flash devices] and tripod, aimed at the audience.* ASSISTANT *has a folder filled with papers, photographs, etc.* ASSISTANT *looks around at the theatre and audience, checking light meter readings. Both* PHOTOGRAPHER *and* ASSISTANT *speak mainly to the audience, and do so in a very natural way that must seem extemporaneous, but in a way which should also, at times, express just as naturally an intense gravity.*

ASSISTANT. Don't be nervous. Just act natural.

PHOTOGRAPHER. *(Fidgeting with camera:)* This should only take a minute. *(Brief pause.)* To make a record of your souls.

ASSISTANT. Don't blink. *(Looking around at the light in the theater, checking a meter reading.)* We may need more light. I don't know, maybe not. *(Brief pause. Pulling a small antique photograph, wrapped in a protective cover, out of a folder. The photograph, though the audience won't really be able to see it, should be of a grotesquely mutilated corpse.)* Anyway, why don't we start.

PHOTOGRAPHER. Good. *(Looks through the viewfinder, sees that lens cap is still on camera, removes it. If there's no lens cap, then he makes an adjustment to the camera.)* Much better.

ASSISTANT. What we're going to be doing here is re-enacting, or re-creating —celebrating, too, really—a little-known photograph by an unknown photographer, depicting—well, you'll see. The title—it's a little hard to make out the writing on the back—the title is "Bully Composition." It was taken in 1898 in Cuba during the Spanish-American War. "The Splendid Little War." I'll pass this around, and, if you look closely, you can see how strangely the people *(She looks at it for the first time and realizes she has the wrong photo.)* —and, oops, wrong one. Sorry. I have it here. Hang on one sec. *(She begins looking through the papers in her folder, just as she is saying "..., wrong one.")* Sorry. *(She continues looking.)*

PHOTOGRAPHER. We'll wait. *(Brief pause. He looks through the viewfinder.)* "People in a Building, Breathing." That's what I'd title this. Or maybe not. *(He looks again. Referring to people in the seats to the side of the stage, should there be any:)* I don't know if we'll get everyone. *(He moves the tripod back a foot or so. Perhaps bumping into the string that decorates the back of the set.)* String. *(To audience seated on the side:)* We're all here in spirit.

ASSISTANT. Sorry. I'm thinking. Just one second.

(During the PHOTOGRAPHER's *lines above,* ASSISTANT *turns a quarter-turn or so, away from the audience, and stares, concentrating on a spot on the floor, trying to remember where she might have left the photograph. This should feel very real and awkward and clumsy, as in life, rather than as in a staged moment of "awkwardness.")*

PHOTOGRAPHER. *(To* ASSISTANT*:)* Maybe I could do my… *(*ASSISTANT, *as she continues to look for the photograph, nods a quick "yes." To audience:)* So, I do a little thing, sort of a—I don't know, you'll see. It seems to be helpful, picture-taking-wise. It helps get people into a kind of—well, I hope it does, anyway—but just, the right place. It's probably weird, but, maybe it'll be good. So, let me give it a try. *(*PHOTOGRAPHER *begins a concerted effort at going into some kind of a trance.)* Private… *(Very long pause.* ASSISTANT *waits, respectfully. She looks, occasionally and very discretely, for the photo. He doesn't go into a trance.)* Sorry. Usually I can do it.

ASSISTANT. And, I don't think we have our photo. Um, maybe it'd be good if we could…one second. *(She whispers something to* PHOTOGRAPHER. *Very short exchange, between them, as they decide to move on. To audience:)* Okay. We're fine. *(Very quick last peek into the folder.)* We can live without it. What you would see, if you could see it, is a group of American troops sitting on the ground and on boxes, staring at the camera. This was San Juan Hill, the Spanish American War, July 1st. The single worst day of fighting, they say, the bloodiest. "Bully Composition." Photographer unknown. The people in it have this sort of historic look in their eyes.

PHOTOGRAPHER. Almost like they were born to be in a photograph. Except, they don't really have any expressions. They're just regular Americans, staring straight ahead. As they—I don't know—as they try to gather the strength their post-photograph lives are going to ask of them.

ASSISTANT. They have expressions. People always have expressions. You just have to look. *(Very brief pause.)* What else. It's black-and-white, of course. They're right there, the people, waiting for you, kind of. One of them looks like he wants to cry but doesn't know what crying is. Or like it's a burden for him to have a face. *(Brief pause.)* Also, there's some discrepancy about the time of day.

PHOTOGRAPHER. *(Somewhat dismissively:)* But it's fairly clear.

ASSISTANT. Well, but there are questions.

PHOTOGRAPHER. *(Conceding the point, somewhat:)* Yes, there are questions. You can't tell from the sky if it's morning or evening. It can look like both.

ASSISTANT. Of course, the sky. But it's not just the sky. It's the meaning of the sky. The meaning of morning or evening and what came in between.

Were they afraid of dying, or, happy to be alive? Did they just do something awful, or were they about to do something brave? One has his legs crossed. He's holding a piece of paper. It's such a simple picture. You'd think we'd be able to tell.

PHOTOGRAPHER. Well, the resolution isn't great. The sky looks like it's almost done in watercolor. And the flag in the background is all blurry. And, I think—is it torn?

ASSISTANT. No. Maybe a little frayed, at the end. But, yeah, blurry.

PHOTOGRAPHER. The rest is very still, sharp, the people. They had to sit like that for a while, because of the old cameras. Imagine. Nobody moving. It's very quiet. Storm clouds and maybe something else are gathering. A mosquito—and this was in the days of malaria—a mosquito lands on your cheek and just sits there. You wait for the click. No birds singing or barking dogs. This was the moment.

ASSISTANT. Yes, but, possibly not; which is the interesting thing. That there can be such precision regarding the actual moment, but, so much confusion regarding the context. Or, regarding the two moments on either side.

PHOTOGRAPHER. I think it's morning.

ASSISTANT. *(To audience, mainly.)* It may be, but, I guess…I don't know. If you could see it, really look into the picture of these people's eyes—God, I wish I had it—I think you'd see a bigger mystery other than just what time it was. Wouldn't you? Had they just come through it all? All the shattered bones and blood and bleeding horses and noise. Or was it still just farm boys' quiet dreams of glory, something fine and right that they were about to do? Which version were they? And what's either one supposed to look like? You'd see it, if you could see it. The confusion, the contradiction, the whole problem. It's there in their faces, somehow, as they sit there, real people with real names, really sitting there, whenever it was. Imagine that. If we could, just for a minute, just feel that: a day, a serious day, or a night, in someone else's life, in someone else's shoes, their dirty wet actual socks. A splinter. Or, homesickness, doubts, cuts and scratches. Someone else's. An unheld hand. A war. Feel that. Look at a picture and feel that. *(Brief pause.)* We should try and learn to look at each other harder. *(Brief pause.)* If we did, well, then, maybe, then, we'd all know… I don't know.

PHOTOGRAPHER. Maybe. *(He makes some adjustment to the camera. Pause. Gently:)* Why don't we try to take this.

ASSISTANT. Take what?

PHOTOGRAPHER. This.

ASSISTANT. But, this *what?* That's what I'm trying to say.

PHOTOGRAPHER. This photograph. Is what I'm trying to say. *(ASSIS-TANT is standing somewhere in the camera's frame. Motioning her to the side.)* Could you... *(She moves.)* And, could you move that light down.

ASSISTANT. It's easy to feel sorry for people in a photograph, to think you understand life, or understand history and war. *(Adjusting the angle of a light:)* It's easy to look at a picture, wince, keep looking, and say you can't look anymore. Like that?

PHOTOGRAPHER. *(PHOTOGRAPHER stares into the light, a little distracted.)* Yes. *(Pause.)* Yeah. Good. It's always a compromise, with light, as to whether you... *(He continues to stare mainly into the light. Pause.)* Private... Private Edward Thomas; Sterling, Indiana. We're halfway up a hill that goes down the other side. Under sickening violent fire. Such insane rage over there. Over here. Mullen lost his eye and he's crying out of the other one. Foley's holding his insides. His intestines look like animals. Somebody lost a hand and it's lying in the dirt in the sun like a drawing. They told us not to shoot or move or make noise. So we're not. Americans, in the chaos and mayhem, lying dead still, quietly dripping sweat or slowly getting sick, hiding on the side of a hill, waiting for orders. Forward or back, I don't care, but, somewhere, soon, please. It's like being in someone else's nightmare. War is not hell, it's not organized enough to be. Then you come home, get your picture in the paper, mangled in body or spirit. One way or the other, mother, the ghost of your boy is coming home. But not now. Still have some time and life to waste, now. I wonder if the hand is Spanish or American. No such thing as locals here. Just us and other foreigners. Poor people from around the world, shooting each other and wishing we were home. I have to pee so badly. I wonder if you will remember me or think of me, ever. A hungry nobody lying on the ground, waiting for a sign, trying not to shake, waiting for the— *(Pause. He comes out of his trance.)* Okay. All right. Good. I think that should...we're good. Maybe down just a tiny bit. *(ASSISTANT, showing both wariness of and concern for the PHOTOGRA-PHER, adjusts the angle of light.)* There.

ASSISTANT. Okay? Is everything...

PHOTOGRAPHER. We're good.

ASSISTANT. So...all right. I think we're ready. *(The following series of lines are all spoken to the audience, most of them very much as if they are "directions" one might give an actor or model whose photo is being taken. Throughout, PHOTOGRA-PHER will be looking through the viewfinder, making adjustments, and surveying the audience.)* So, okay, "Bully Composition." Here we go. There you are.

PHOTOGRAPHER. *(Looking through viewfinder.)* There you are.

ASSISTANT. *(To the audience:)* Is it morning or evening?

PHOTOGRAPHER. It's morning.

ASSISTANT. It might be evening.

PHOTOGRAPHER. *(Making a small adjustment to the camera. Returning to viewfinder:)* You're just sitting there. All is quiet.

ASSISTANT. Or is it. Even The Hundred Years' War had a middle. A little quiet moment in the middle that somehow determined the end. *(She holds for a moment, to allow for a "little quiet moment.")* Like maybe that.

PHOTOGRAPHER. *(Green smoke starts to come out onto the stage. Looking through the viewfinder.)* Good. Nice. I don't know what the smoke is. I think it's for something else. Don't pay any attention. I'm sure it's fine. Just be you.

ASSISTANT. On the threshold of death.

PHOTOGRAPHER. Just act natural.

ASSISTANT. You're sitting on a wooden box. There's a war going on. A real war. The blurry flag gently waves. Maybe you're about to be shot in the throat. *(Quietly, plainly:)* Bang. *(Brief pause.)* Splendid.

PHOTOGRAPHER. Good. *(Looking through viewfinder.)* I think this is good. *(He looks again.)* It's almost better.

ASSISTANT. It is kind of a perfect... I mean, it's really even more... What if there were never any photograph? "Bully Composition." And this is it, now. You are it, now. God, look at you. If you could see yourselves. What are you in the middle of? How do you want to be remembered? What do you want people to see in your eyes?

PHOTOGRAPHER. Just sit up nice and straight. *(To someone in the audience wearing glasses:)* Maybe you could take your glasses off. Or, no, they're good. *(To* ASSISTANT*:)* Keep going.

ASSISTANT. Are you afraid of dying or happy to be alive? The fighting, the horror, the glory, our country—is it over or has it not even started? Show us the national dilemma, in your faces. A little anthem in your eyes. It's beautiful. Your anxieties, your agonies. Very photogenic. *(Referring to some people five or six rows back:)* Are you're getting these—

PHOTOGRAPHER. *(Interrupting:)* Yeah, thanks. They're great. Thanks everyone. Almost there.

ASSISTANT. Just a little more. Feel more things. Think bigger things. This'll be you, someday. Gorgeous. If you could see the strange light in your eyes. And the dividedness. You're going to break my heart. *(To* PHOTOGRAPHER*:)* Is this—

PHOTOGRAPHER. *(Interrupting:)* Yes. Almost. A little more.

ASSISTANT. Be historical.

PHOTOGRAPHER. Good. *(To a particular person in the audience, in response to his or her expression:)* Very nice, keep that, keep that.

ASSISTANT. Show us you, trying to be better, mortally afraid.

PHOTOGRAPHER. *(Making adjustments to camera, exposure settings, etc.:)* What a beautiful people. So calm-looking. Last chance. Almost, almost...

ASSISTANT. Be more unknowing. More forgiving. More mortal. Try to be more mortal. As much as you can stand.

PHOTOGRAPHER. *(He looks up from the viewfinder.)* Perfect. *(Camera flash. Blackout.)*

End of Play

Brian Avers and Bess Wohl in *Szinhaz*
Naked Angels at The Duke in New York City (2007).

SZINHAZ
by Itamar Moses

BIOGRAPHY

Itamar Moses is the author of the full-length plays *Outrage, Bach At Leipzig, Celebrity Row, The Four of Us, Yellowjackets, Back Back Back,* and *Completeness,* and various short plays and one-acts. He is presently adapting Jonathan Lethem's *The Fortress Of Solitude.* His work has appeared Off-Broadway and elsewhere in New York, at regional theatres across the country and in Canada, and has been published by Faber & Faber, Heinemann Press, Playscripts Inc., Samuel French, Inc., and Vintage. He has received new play commissions from The McCarter Theater, Playwrights Horizons, Berkeley Repertory Theatre, The Wilma Theater, Manhattan Theatre Club, and South Coast Rep Repertory. Mr. Moses holds an MFA in Dramatic Writing from NYU and has taught playwriting at Yale and NYU. He is a member of the Dramatists Guild, MCC Playwrights Coalition, Naked Angels Mag 7, and is a New York Theatre Workshop Usual Suspect. He was born in Berkeley, California, and now lives in Brooklyn, New York.

ACKNOWLEDGMENTS

Szinhaz was first produced by Naked Angels at The Duke in New York City as a part of *Armed and Naked in America* (April 11–22, 2007). It was directed by Michelle Tattenbaum with the following cast:

MARIE .... Bess Wohl
ISTVAN .... Brian Avers

And the following production staff:

Producers .... Andy Donald
                                                                           Dan Klores
Scenic Design .... David Rockwell
Lighting Design .... Jason Lyons
Costume Design .... Jessica Wegener
Sound Design .... Drew Levy, Tony Smolenski IV
Projection Design .... Batwin and Robin Productions, Inc.

CAST OF CHARACTERS

MARIE
ISTVAN

SZINHAZ

Two chairs. In one, ISTVAN, *bearded, wearing black. In the other,* MA-
RIE, *lovely, holding a stack of index cards.*

MARIE. Hello, Americans. Welcome very much to our special talk today
talking with the very special and interesting director Istvan Zoltan Andras.
Who will talk with us about his work which is some of the most special
and interesting work in the whole of former Soviet Union. Some of it that
we will be talking about will be in not English. When he is speaking. And
I will try to make it for you in English. And my English is very bad. It will
be for you very painful. For you to listen to it. But if you try, hopefully, you
will get used to it.

Okay! So! Here sitting next to me now is, you know him, and who is he
already, which is the reason you are coming here, but I will say one things
or two things about him also in case of you forgot it.

He is borned beneath the Soviets at what was a very bad and terrible time
in which there was no freedoms. And this was very very painful. For him
and for all of us. But we got used to it.

Next, after he growed up some little bits, he wented through training at our
Theatre Institute of Academy of Drama Studies. Here a director is practicing
first by working very much in a room alone with no actors.

After this, Istvan is starting his own company, the name of it, in English,
it's not so easy, em, *The Slow Death of the Human Soul.* This company is now
of course very much knowed about by peoples, but for very much time it
was not knowed, or if it was, it was unliked, and not liked, which is what
people were saying in the audiences, and in the critics, and also shouting in
the streets at Istvan. Until he growed up some little bits more and made his
very special production of a play by Anton Pavlovich Chekhov, who, you
know who is he, of his play, em, *There Are Sisters And There Are Three Of
Them.* Yes? And this production have such realism that it make his reputa-
tion for genius. But because Istvan does not care by now about this, by
now, and so was unable to enjoy it, this success, too, he found very painful.

Okay! So! I have here the questions that you wroted down for him before.
On index card. And because Istvan can hear English more better than he
can speak it, I will read it loud, and he can think about it. And then he will
answer. And I will say for you.

*(*MARIE *looks at the index card on the top of the pile.)*

MARIE. The question is: "Have you ever and or would you ever direct
outside of your own company?"

261

(ISTVAN *speaks in his own language. Her translations can overlap slightly with his speech, organically, as needed, sometimes checking in with him, whatever feels right.*)

MARIE. Yes, Istvan has worked without *The Slow Death of the Human Soul* three times. And each time it was very different from the other times.

(ISTVAN *speaks in his own language.*)

MARIE. The first time it was in Vienna with a very special and interesting company there called *Time Will Destroy Your Capacity To Love.*

(ISTVAN *speaks in his own language.*)

MARIE. And it was terrible.

(ISTVAN *speaks in his own language.*)

MARIE. It was like being punched.

(ISTVAN *speaks in his own language.*)

MARIE. Again and again and again.

(ISTVAN *speaks in his own language.*)

MARIE. Into his face.

(ISTVAN *speaks in his own language.*)

MARIE. By a train.

(ISTVAN *speaks in his own language.*)

MARIE. And this was because this company is having its own director who is with Istvan, em, rivalizating? Yes? They are making rivals with each other? And Istvan cannot work this way. Rivalizating with another man.

(ISTVAN *speaks in his own language.*)

MARIE. And so was exposed in front of collaborators and later audiences to only, em, humiliation.

(ISTVAN *speaks in his own language.*)

MARIE. And ridicule.

(ISTVAN *speaks in his own language.*)

MARIE. And also, how do you call them, projectiles.

(ISTVAN *speaks in his own language.*)

MARIE. Which was at first very painful.

(ISTVAN *speaks in his own language.*)

MARIE. But he got used to it.

(ISTVAN *speaks in his own language.*)

MARIE. The second time it was in Italy. In Roma.

(ISTVAN *speaks in his own language.*)

MARIE. And this time it was horrible.

(ISTVAN speaks in his own language.)

MARIE. Like being kicked in his groins.

(ISTVAN speaks in his own language.)

MARIE. Forever.

(ISTVAN speaks in his own language.)

MARIE. And this was because the actors inside Italy could not understand what Istvan is telling to them.

(ISTVAN speaks in his own language.)

MARIE. So they do whatever it is that they want.

(ISTVAN speaks in his own language.)

MARIE. And also there is much money and a big stage and big things flying.

(ISTVAN speaks in his own language.)

MARIE. But all of it means nothing.

(ISTVAN speaks in his own language.)

MARIE. And this was very painful.

(ISTVAN speaks in his own language.)

MARIE. But he got used to it.

(ISTVAN speaks in his own language.)

MARIE. The third time was the most different of all. When he goes to Moscow.

(ISTVAN speaks in his own language.)

MARIE. And this was extremely bad.

(A moment. ISTVAN doesn't say anything else. A moment. MARIE moves the index card to the back of the pile. She reads the new one on top. Glances at ISTVAN and back at the cards. Moves the new card to the back. Reads the next one. Moves it to the back. Finally sees one she likes.)

MARIE. The question is: "I saw your Chekhov production last winter. And I was intrigued by how were able to work without a set or any other design elements and also to eliminate much of the text. Why did you make this choice?"

(ISTVAN speaks in his own language.)

MARIE. Our play last winter was the Chekhov, em, *The Animal Which is Flying in Circles Over the Ocean but Near to the Beach…? And Enjoys Garbage and is a Kind of a Bird…?* Yes? You know it? So this was the play.

(ISTVAN speaks in his own language.)

MARIE. First when we are working on it he thinks that we will require lights and sound noises and things like this that one will have most of the time.

(ISTVAN speaks in his own language.)

MARIE. But then he realized something.

(ISTVAN speaks in his own language.)

MARIE. Oh! Which he will demonstrate by taking right now a small pause in front of you.

(ISTVAN speaks in his own language.)

MARIE. A small silence.

(ISTVAN speaks in his own language.)

MARIE. In which there will be no talking in it.

ISTVAN. Now.

(A silence. Long enough to feel it. However long feels like it might be too long and a little longer than that. They don't move.)

(Then, at last, finally, ISTVAN speaks in his own language.)

MARIE. Okay! So!

(ISTVAN speaks in his own language.)

MARIE. This silence that we just have. It is very boring.

(ISTVAN speaks in his own language.)

MARIE. Probably you are very bored during it and while it is going on.

(ISTVAN speaks in his own language.)

MARIE. Or perhaps after a few moments you began to fantasize sexually.

(ISTVAN speaks in his own language.)

MARIE. He did.

(ISTVAN speaks in his own language. A moment. MARIE speaks back to him, gently scolding. ISTVAN insists, in his own language, that she translate. She sighs.)

MARIE. He thought about this woman here in the first row, hello, and how much and in how many different ways he would like to make love with her.

(ISTVAN speaks in his own language. A moment.)

MARIE. Perhaps finishing with an ejaculation.

(ISTVAN repeats his last few words. The translation was incomplete.)

MARIE. Into her face.

(ISTVAN speaks in his own language.)

MARIE. Which at first might be painful.

(ISTVAN *speaks in his own language.*)

MARIE. But she will get used to it.

(ISTVAN *speaks in his own language.*)

MARIE. And so this was very entertaining to think about it.

(ISTVAN *speaks in his own language.*)

MARIE. But it was necessary. Because the small silence that we had here was too boring to exist inside of it without feeling, how do you say it…? A stillness in the earth that deprives us of all meaning. Yes?

(ISTVAN *speaks in his own language.*)

MARIE. But now he will tell you few things.

(ISTVAN *speaks in his own language.*)

MARIE. Probably you think that I, sitting here next to him, am here only to translate, and am selected because I know some small bad English, and also it is pleasing to look on me.

(ISTVAN *speaks in his own language.*)

MARIE. But actually I am also one of the actress in Istvan company so that I work with him and was his Nina in the play of the *Garbage Bird,* and one also of the *Triangle of Sisters,* and so on, so on.

(ISTVAN *speaks in his own language.* MARIE *sighs. Knows better than to object.*)

MARIE. And also we are lovers.

(ISTVAN *speaks in his own language.*)

MARIE. For many many years.

(ISTVAN *speaks in his own language.*)

MARIE. Since I am first working with him he loves me from my audition.

(ISTVAN *speaks in his own language.*)

MARIE. Which he remembers it so clear like it is happening still now.

(ISTVAN *speaks in his own language.*)

MARIE. He loves me so much.

(ISTVAN *speaks in his own language.*)

MARIE. He did not know it was possible so much to love a person.

(ISTVAN *speaks in his own language.*)

MARIE. And, in truth, when he was young, he was without any talent whatsoever, and he only make himself into himself for me, to become one that he thinks I can love.

(ISTVAN *speaks in his own language.*)

MARIE. And so never can there be for him work again or love again apart from he looks on me and sees me.

(ISTVAN *speaks in his own language.* MARIE *looks at* ISTVAN. *Then turns back.*)

MARIE. But there is problem.

(ISTVAN *speaks in his own language.*)

MARIE. And. It is problem that I think he does not know.

(ISTVAN *speaks in his own language.*)

MARIE. But he knows it.

(ISTVAN *speaks in his own language. A small silence.* MARIE *says something very quietly to* ISTVAN. *He stares at her, impassive. A moment.*)

MARIE. That I am being with also another man.

(ISTVAN *speaks in his own language.*)

MARIE. One of the actors of the company.

(ISTVAN *speaks in his own language.*)

MARIE. From some months now. Maybe even from a whole year. He does not know exact the time.

(ISTVAN *speaks in his own language.*)

MARIE. And that I am falling perhaps in love with this man.

(ISTVAN *speaks in his own language.*)

MARIE. This man who he, Istvan, brought together with me, in many scenes, and using his skill to make for us a connection.

(ISTVAN *speaks in his own language.*)

MARIE. Causing this horrible disaster for himself.

(ISTVAN *speaks in his own language.*)

MARIE. He knows this. And now I know it that he knows it.

(ISTVAN *speaks in his own language.*)

MARIE. And now he gives to me a choice.

(ISTVAN *speaks in his own language.*)

MARIE. That I can stay with this man. And both of us will be made to go away from the company.

(ISTVAN *speaks in his own language.*)

MARIE. Or to stay with the company. But to stop with the other man and to love only Istvan.

(ISTVAN *speaks in his own language.*)

MARIE. And now he would like to make a second pause now.

(ISTVAN *speaks in his own language.*)

MARIE. To see how this one feels.

(ISTVAN speaks in his own language.)

MARIE. Not like a soul frozen.

(ISTVAN speaks in his own language.)

MARIE. But with motion forward for the soul.

(ISTVAN speaks in his own language.)

MARIE. Which, even though this motion is towards, how do you call...? The endless grave? This movement, it is better than the stillness of the other pause before.

(ISTVAN speaks in his own language.)

MARIE. That it cannot be escaped.

(ISTVAN speaks in his own language.)

MARIE. But that there is no reason to escape it.

(ISTVAN speaks in his own language.)

MARIE. And yes. It will be very painful.

(ISTVAN speaks in his own language. MARIE looks at him. Shakes her head. Looks away from him.)

(A long silence. He stares at her. She stares away.)

(Finally she turns back. And looks at him.)

(Fade to black.)

End of Play